CREATING CHRISTMAS MEMORIES

Family Traditions for a Lifetime

by

CHERI FULLER

HONOR

Tulsa, Oklahoma

2nd Printing
Over 12,000 in Print

Creating Christmas Memories — Family Traditions for a Lifetime
ISBN 1-56292-851-1

P. O. Box 770493
Oklahoma City, Oklahoma 73177

Published by Honor Books
P. O. Box 55388
Tulsa, Oklahoma 74155-1388

Printed in the United States of America.

CONTENTS

To Holmes,
who loves Christmas and
whose generous heart
loves to give.

My thanks to the people and families who graciously shared their traditions and ideas: Patty Johnston, Melanie Hemry, Charlotte Foreman, Jeanne Edwards, Posy Lough, Mary Mayer, Melina Shellenberger, Gail Schoellkopf, Dorothy Burshek, Candy Snowbarger, Ellene Powell, Gudbjorg Chesnut, Dana Myers, Kay Bishop, Laura Neely and her grandmother, Thelma Randall, Diane Allen, Penny Hook, Charlotte Marcus, Marianne Adkins, Lori Turpen, Caroline Oda, the Tom McWhorter family, and the Jordan family. Special thanks to Keith Provance for his encouragement of this project and editor Jimmy Peacock and his family. And, of course, I am grateful to the Heath family and the entire Fuller family with whom I have enjoyed many traditions and special Christmases.

TREASURES OF THE HEART

The Value of Building Family Traditions at Christmas

I have great confidence in the revelations which holidays bring forth.
Benjamin Disraeli

Tramping out to the farm to cut down a fresh Christmas tree, making a gingerbread house or homemade cookies with bright red and green sprinkles, reading the Christmas story aloud from the Bible surrounded by lighted candles, joining with one another on Christmas Eve to sing "Silent Night" — all these kinds of family traditions are treasures of the heart, enjoyed together in the present and cherished over and over in our memories as we grow up, marry, and begin our own families.

We may not realize that something we do is a tradition until our child asks, "What do you mean, we're not going to carol at the nursing home this year?" or until our teenager says, "What? No time to drive out and see the lights at Ski Island! It won't be Christmas without that!"

Traditions are formed delicately, sometimes without our realizing it. An experience that brings such joy that we want to repeat it in the same way soon becomes a family custom.

Holiday traditions are part of a quilt of memories that reach all the way back to our childhoods. In my own case, I remember Christmas mornings spent under our green pine tree covered with old-fashioned glass balls, multi-colored bulbs, and lots of silvery tinsel which seemed to dance in the warm, soft light. (In spite of Mom's oft-repeated exhortation to carefully place just a few strands of tinsel on each branch, we kids always delighted in tossing it on in clumps).

In one of my favorite holiday photos, all five of us sisters are sitting under the tree holding new dolls (all except Diana, that is, who proudly displays her new Monopoly game). I loved the beautiful doll clothes that Mom had sewed especially for my new Christmas doll. I remember our five red stockings, plus baby brother George's stocking, that held apples, oranges, tangerines, and sticky candy. And Mom always found time for Christmas giving to people who wouldn't otherwise have a merry Christmas — like shiny new shoes for children at the orphans' home and a holiday food basket for a needy family. I can almost smell the mouth-watering traditional Christmas dinner complete with orange and coconut ambrosia, sweet potato pie, turkey and giblet gravy. In my memory I can also still hear the traditional wrangling over who was going to get the coveted drumsticks!

Being in a warm climate can have its own special memories. Caroline Oda and her family live in Hawaii, and she writes, "When we have a holiday or open house, we do our feasting out on the lanai (patio) in the cool breezes. Every year a group of Christmas carolers come around in a horse-drawn street car and serenade us. Teenagers go down to the beach and build a fire and sing Christmas carols. The business district of Honolulu is all lighted up and people park their cars on the edge of town and stroll through the cool evenings to see all the scenes. We stand out under the stars on Christmas Eve waiting to go into the candlelight service and worship the Lord."

For any family, large or small, two-parent or single-parent, traditions are an important way to build a sense of continuity and security. Traditions help make up the glue that holds families together. In times of death, loss, moving, and inevitable change, traditions bind us together.

"How do we keep our balance?" asks Tevye, the Jewish dairyman in the beloved musical play and film, *Fiddler on the Roof.*

"Tradition!" he rightly concludes. "Without tradition, our lives would be as shaky as a fiddler on a roof."

So too in our day, tradition helps us keep our balance. In this world of rapid changes, ceaseless mobility, and constant uncertainty, family traditions serve to steady our lives and keep us on course.

On a cold December evening in Maine, the temperature was falling as thick, white snowflakes swirled outside the windows of our rented house on Sligo Road. Inside a pot of hot chili simmered on the stove and the sounds of Music Box Christmas tunes rang out as we opened boxes of our "memory ornaments" and got ready to decorate the woodsy-smelling New England pine.

We had recently moved two thousand miles away from family, friends, and the usual December happenings in our church and community. We missed them, of course, but the traditions we had shared in the past and enjoyed again that season helped us and our three children to draw together in a bond of warmth and security which saw us through a cold environment many miles from "home."

Like the perennial flower that blooms once a year to give us joy, the traditions we share together each year remind us of who we are and where we have been as a family. Family customs handed down from past generations, journeys we have taken together, close personal relationships with friends, the sharing in the heritage of other countries and cultures different from our own, all these traditions — old and new — weave our lives together into a tapestry of memories that will last for a lifetime and beyond.

CREATE A QUILT OF MEMORIES
to keep me warm.
An inner warmth that comes
from light of happy times.
Weave in the threads of holidays,
of friends and families...
Delights of seashore, fields,
of city parks.
The simplest happenings
traced out in love
become a pattern,
for my quilt of memories.[1]
Ruth Reardon

[1]Permission to quote from *Listening to the Littlest* copyright © 1984 Ruth Reardon granted by C.R. Gibson, Publisher. All rights reserved.

The word *tradition* implies the handing down of stories, beliefs, rituals, and customs from generation to generation. So traditions can be a wonderful tool in teaching and transferring values to our children. With family Christmas traditions we share the importance of Christ's coming and His love for each of us. We pass on to our children and grandchildren, values and standards like kindness, unselfishness, generosity, gratitude, and respect for others.

Children have a deep need to belong, and if they don't find fulfillment of that need in the right places — like at home and in the midst of a loving family — then they will look for it in the wrong places. Family traditions can help provide that sense of belonging which youngsters need, at the same time helping them to develop a healthy self-esteem as they become aware of their own family's unique heritage and customs. Talking dolls, Nintendo games, and electronic gadgets may get lost or broken, but memories — especially those of warmth and togetherness — last for a lifetime. As children grow up and leave home, they continue to keep within them a strong sense of belonging as they recall and observe family traditions which they in turn pass along to their own young families.

Shared experiences also involve children with happenings, people, lifestyles, and other cultures, giving them the opportunity to participate and share in the lives of others outside the immediate family. Traditions help form foundations for learning. Thus, this book includes many traditions in which children can take an active part and enjoy as much as grownups.

In a survey, thousands of school children were asked what they thought makes a happy family. The kids didn't answer a big house, designer jeans, new cars, or CD players. The most frequently mentioned key to happiness was doing things together.[2]

Thus, the focus in this collection of Christmas traditions is on doing things together as a family, on giving rather than getting, on preparing our hearts for Christmas, on building relationships with loved ones and friends, on reaching out to others outside our home and church and culture, and on using our imagination and creativity.

---

[2]Paraphrased from *The Magic of Encouragement* by Stephanie Marston (New York: William Morrow & Company, 1990), p. 86.

CREATING CHRISTMAS MEMORIES

Christmas is a wonderful time to establish new traditions, enhance old ones, and build special memories. The "treasures of the heart" found in the following pages will include traditions for you to begin, or to add to your list of old favorite ones, but most of all for you and your family to enjoy *together* now.

CHAPTER ONE

ADVENT TRADITIONS

Christmas Is Coming!
Christmas. . . the season of gifts
great and small
When joy is the nicest
gift of them all.

Anonymous

Advent begins on the fourth Sunday before Christmas and continues until Christmas Day. The term *advent* is derived from the Latin word *adventus* meaning "arrival" and refers to a coming of some type. In the Christian calendar, Advent is a time of preparation for the coming of Christ and making room for Him in our hearts and homes.

At the beginning of December some families get out special Christmas dishes to use during the holiday month. The pile of favorite Christmas books comes out of the depths of the closet or the far reaches of the attic to be lovingly placed into a decorated basket by the tree. The family Christmas photo album is once again proudly displayed on the coffee table. The traditional nativity scene is brought out of its worn cardboard box and carefully set up among the greenery on the mantelpiece. And warm Christmas music is played throughout the house. Christmas is coming!

One way to prepare as a family is by setting aside and observing special celebration, activity, and devotional times. The Advent traditions which follow will build memories and get you and your household ready for Christmas.

CHRISTMAS ALBUM

The Christmas album is a special place to keep all of your Christmas keepsake photographs so you don't have to wonder each year, "Where is the photo of the children sitting on Santa's knee?" or, "Where's that picture of Dad putting together the bicycle, and Granddad setting up the train set?"

Every year my family and I get out our green satin-covered Christmas album and place it on the coffee table. When we first received it from Joan, my husband's mom, we put in a few old pictures of Holmes and me under our own childhood Christmas trees, and then added photos of our first Christmas as newlyweds, the children's first Christmases, and so on through the years. The pictures include special events, school plays, and friends who came over for holiday gatherings. The album is a real joy to look through during the days of Advent and to add to each year.

To make a special family Christmas album, take a standard or large photo album and cover it in some bright holiday fabric. You can use any material — red or green or white, fancy satin or country print. You could embroider the word *Christmas* diagonally across the cover by hand or machine before placing it on the album.

Each day during Advent, you can add letters to Santa, bright ideas for the future, and those Christmas treasures which you will share together as a family during the coming weeks of the Christmas season.

CHRISTMAS JOURNAL

A Christmas journal or memory notebook is easy to keep. Each year record anything about the Christmas holiday that you would like to recall in the years to come. Include everything of interest — from the weather at the time, to what gifts each member received and the activities you engaged in as a family group.

Each person who wants to can write what was unique about this particular holiday, about a special trip that was taken, or about a humorous happening that took place during the season.

(For ideas on beginning a Christmas journal, see the recollections section at the end of the book.)

CHRISTMAS STRAW

This special Advent tradition encourages unselfishness and provides opportunities for showing love to family members in practical ways.

First, straw is collected and placed in a big basket by the side of an empty cradle representing a manger. (You could use a basket or a doll crib for the manger and place straw beside it.) On the first day of December, the family draws names. Each week on Sunday, new names are drawn. For the person whose name is drawn, during the coming week one kind or thoughtful deed is done each day without his knowing it (like making his bed for him while he is in the shower or polishing his shoes while he is at work).

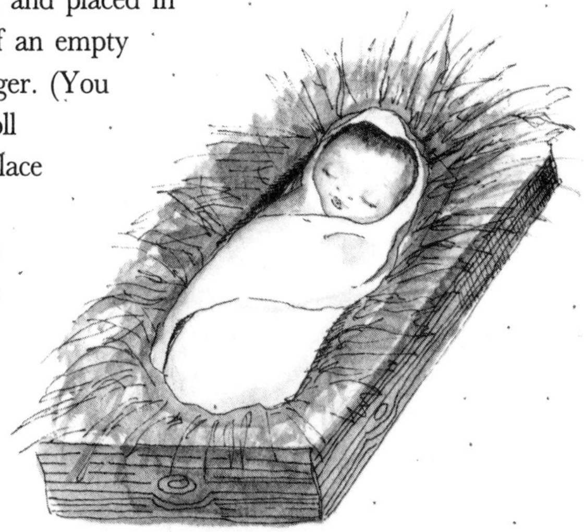

These acts of kindness have nothing to do with money or "storebought" gifts. Instead they are ways of noticing the needs of others and helping to meet those needs quietly and unobtrusively. They may include something as simple as sending an encouraging note to the secret "person of the week."

Each time someone in the family does a kind or thoughtful deed, he gets to place a bit of straw in the manger. Ideally, by Christmas Eve, Baby Jesus (a doll wrapped in a "swaddling blanket") has a cradle full of straw on which to lie!

(A smaller version of the Christmas Straw manger can be fashioned from a piece of cardboard or poster paper. To this miniature crib is added one piece of straw for each act of kindness during Advent. For directions on how to make the diminutive cradle, see the resource list at the end of the book.)

ADVENT HEIRLOOM STOCKING

The Lough family in Connecticut has a wonderful tradition using a stocking made from their son Kyser's baby carrier cover. On the front side of the stocking they sew twenty-four ribbons and on each one they place a memento from Kyser's baby days up to the present year. Every day, beginning on the first of December, the family takes one item out of the stocking, tells the story behind it, and ties it to one of the brightly colored ribbons on the outside of the stocking. The number of empty ribbons tells the number of days until Christmas. When Christmas Day arrives, the stocking is empty and ready to be filled with treats and surprises.

To make an Advent heirloom stocking for your child, you can use swatches taken from a favorite blanket, snowsuit, or quilt, or just bright, colorful fabric. You may even want to purchase a ready-made stocking to which you add the twenty-four ribbons. The mementoes you choose to place inside the stocking can be anything from the child's first rattle to a Brownie or Cub Scout award or even a small souvenir of a memorable trip. Change the mementoes each year as the child grows and develops.

(For more information about making an Advent heirloom stocking and turning everyday items into ornaments that are family treasures, see the "Posy Collection" in the resource section at the back of this book.)

ADVENT CALENDAR

The time draws near the birth of Christ;
The moon is hid; the night is still;
The Christmas bells from hill to hill
Answer each other in the mist.
Alfred, Lord Tennyson

An Advent calendar contains reminders each day that Christmas is coming. Most Advent calendars contain a set of tiny doors to open, one for each day leading up to Christmas Day. Behind each door is a picture of a person, scene, or object having to do with the season or the birth of the Christ Child. Since the season of Advent does not have exactly the same number of days each year, many commercial Advent calendars have twenty-four doors, one for each day in December before Christmas.

ADVENT WREATH

The Advent wreath is the center of many family celebrations during the weeks before Christmas. The Advent wreath is a circle, usually made of styrofoam or grapevine, covered with evergreen foliage, with places for four or five candles. The evergreen wreath, which can be made or purchased, is set flat on a platter, tray or table.

The colors of the candles may vary: four purple or white, or three purple and one rose or pink candle. According to one tradition, a purple candle is lit on the first Sunday of Advent and relit each following day until Christmas. A second purple candle is lit on the second Sunday in Advent, and so on until all the four candles have been lit. If a rose or pink candle is used, it is first lit on the third Sunday in Advent. In this version, the three purple candles represent the Three Wise Men and the rose or pink candle represents the Virgin Mary.

A recent development in Advent wreathes is the placing of a Christmas candle — usually a large white taper — in the center of the wreath, which is lit on Christmas Eve at midnight.

Another version of the Advent wreath has five candleholders set into the greenery for Advent candles. The circle shape of the wreath represents God's eternal love, and each candle is symbolic of Christ, the light of the world.

Another interpretation of the significance of the candles is as follows:

The first Sunday's candle is the Prophet's candle — representing *hope.*

The second Sunday's candle is the Bethlehem candle — representing *faith.*

The third candle is the Shepherd's candle — symbolizing *joy.*

The fourth Sunday's candle is the Angel's candle — symbolizing *peace.*

The fifth candle is the Christ's candle — which stands for *love.*

Whichever of the traditional wreathes you choose, on each of the four Sunday evenings in Advent (or on another evening during the week) you and your family can sit in a circle, light a new candle, and relight the ones from the previous weeks. (Children can take turns lighting the candles and blowing them out.) Or you could use the Advent wreath as your table centerpiece.

You can have a family devotional — reading a Scripture or a text from a devotional guide, singing a Christmas carol, and closing with sentence prayers. Or you can create your own family Advent celebration each Sunday with the theme focusing on what that particular day's candle symbolizes. Then at midnight on Christmas Eve (or on Christmas morning), you can light the Christ's candle, celebrating the birth of the Savior.

Advent family celebrations are a special time of togetherness and worship which focuses on the real meaning of Christmas.

THE NATIVITY SCENE

Carefully stored away during the rest of the year, the nativity figures of Mary and Joseph, Baby Jesus, the angel, shepherds, wise men and animals are lovingly unwrapped and gently placed on the piano, mantel, or table, a visual reminder of the Christmas story.

Young children particularly enjoy reenacting the story while moving the figures about. The nativity scene can thus be used as part of your weekly family Advent devotions:

The first week, put down straw for the manger scene. The second week, put up the empty stable and arrange the animals in it. The third week, set the figures of Mary and Joseph a short distance from the stable, moving them a bit closer each day. The fourth week, set the shepherds away from the stable. On Christmas Eve, move Mary and Joseph into the stable beside the manger, place the Christ Child in the manger, and bring the angel, shepherds, and Wise Men onto the scene.

(See the resource list for information on how to order a hands-on nativity set you and your child can make together.)

CHRISTMAS CLUES

The joy of this tradition lasts the whole month long and adds to the anticipation of the coming holiday. In a basket place twenty-five pieces of paper numbered for the days of December (1-25). On each piece of paper is written that day's surprise or special activity to do together as a family:

"Today we get to go out to the farm and cut down our Christmas tree!"

"Today we make our Christmas cookies!"

"Today we go shopping for Grandmother's gift!"

One day the paper clue may lead to another clue and another hidden somewhere in the house, and then to a new Christmas tree ornament or a new Christmas music tape to listen to.

An interesting variation of the "Christmas surprise" is to make each clue be for something to do together *to help someone else:*

"Today we are going to the inner city mission and take warm mittens!"

"Today we are taking a little Christmas cactus plant we have grown to Mrs. Waters (an elderly neighbor)!"

"Today we pick a card from the Salvation Army tree at the mall and make some underprivileged child's Christmas wish come true!"

This way children — and adults — are reminded of the true spirit of Christmas.

"CHRISTMAS IS COMING" PAPER CHAIN

Another good way to help young children understand and appreciate the fact that Christmas is coming (and to count down the remaining days in eager anticipation!) is by helping them to make an Advent paper chain.

First get some red and green construction paper. Cut the paper into equal-sized strips, about one inch wide and eight inches long. On each strip write a simple, enjoyable pre-Christmas activity like, "Make an ornament today," "Make cookies today," "Go see the Christmas lights tonight."

Bring the end of two strips (a red one and a green one) together and tape or staple. Slip another strip through this ring and tape or staple. Continue alternating red and green links until you have made twenty-five of them.

Each day the child tears off a link and does the activity until — one by one — all the loops are gone and it's Christmas Day!

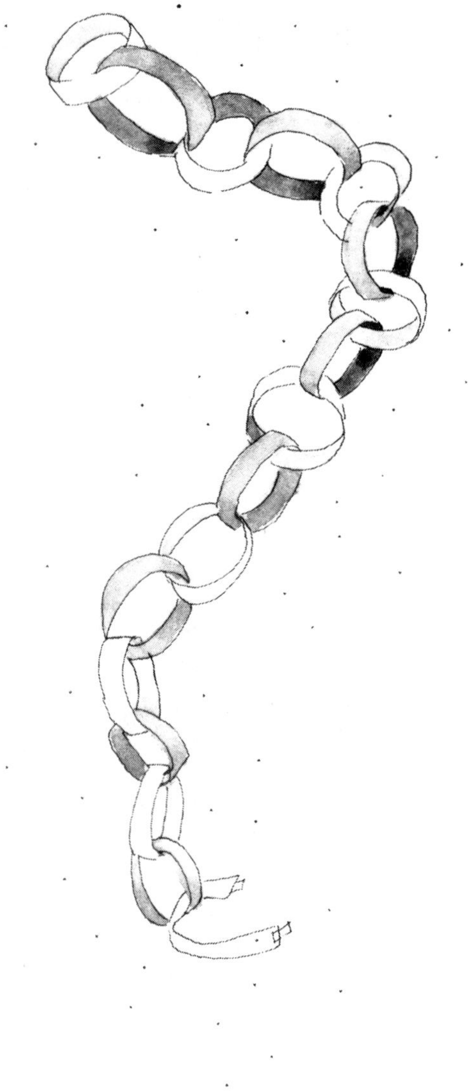

CHAPTER TWO

TREE-TRIMMING TRADITIONS: FAMILY ORNAMENTS, HOUSE-DECORATING, AND PROJECTS

The spirit of Christmas
brings memories
drifting down like snowflakes.

Dorothy Colgan

History tells us that five hundred years ago Martin Luther, leader of the Protestant Reformation, began the custom of decorating Christmas trees.

While walking through the woods one beautiful starry night near Christmas Eve, Luther was struck with a sudden inspiration. Cutting down a small pine tree, he brought it home with him, where he decorated it with lighted candles which he told his wife and children represented Christ as the Light of the World. From that small, seemingly insignificant beginning, the popular custom of decorating trees quickly spread throughout Europe and later was brought to America. Early trees were also decorated with small candies, cookies, and paper and glass ornaments.

Carefully picked and trimmed with tiny twinkling lights — festooned with ornaments from the children's first Christmas, from friends in Germany and across the country, as well as those fashioned by our own hands and collected during our travels throughout the world — our family Christmas tree is more than just a decoration in the living room; it's full of Christmas memories and shines forth as a symbol of love and friendship. The beautiful evergreen tree also symbolizes eternal life.

Choosing just the right tree, bringing it home, and decorating it together as a family can be one of the best parts of the entire Christmas season.

O CHRISTMAS TREE!

One of our fondest memories has been a family outing to a tree farm to select and cut down our Christmas tree. Although there are some geographic limitations, if such an outing is possible in your area, it is well worth the extra time and expense. Before Thanksgiving you can ask at area nurseries or the agricultural extension center at a local college for the location of tree farms in your vicinity. When my family was living in Maine, there was no shortage of Christmas tree farms, but in much of Oklahoma (where we now live) it's a different story.

If the weather permits, you can take along a picnic lunch to enjoy before or after finding your tree. You can also take advantage of the trip to the country to look for pine cones and other seasonal greenery to bring home and use to decorate the house.

LIVING CHRISTMAS TREE

You could help our environment by planting a live Christmas tree this season! Purchase a living Christmas tree, bring it home and decorate it in the usual manner. After Christmas is over, take the tree and plant it in the yard or in a special place in the community where a tree is especially needed.

TREE-TRIMMING NIGHT

In our family we serve the same kind of treats each year on the night we trim the tree, and the children always look forward to it. Our favorite is hot cider, sugar cookies and popcorn, but other possibilities for tree-trimming treats include: "s'mores" (delicious "sandwiches" made with gooey roasted marshmallows and melted Hershey bars scrunched between layers of crispy Graham crackers) and hot cider; cups of hot clam chowder or chili and goldfish crackers; cranberry muffins and cranapple juice; or gingerbread and hot chocolate.

In the warm, sunny climate of Hawaii the Oda family traditionally serves a festive cold soup, French bread, soft cheeses and other French-style hors d'oeuvres to celebrate the French side of their heritage on tree-trimming night.

That's the first night we get out our holiday music tapes from years past — like the Nutcracker Suite, New England Christmastide, Music Box Christmas, and others — and play them while decorating the tree and then throughout the month of December.

Every year on this evening, when our children were small, each child was presented with a special ornament, either handmade or purchased, and had a small box with his or her name on it in which to keep the growing collection of shiny baubles. When Justin, Chris, and Alison are grown and begin their own households, the ornaments will go with them to be used to trim their own family trees.

HOMEMADE ORNAMENTS

The first year Holmes and I were married, we had no ornaments for our tree, and money was very tight. So my friend Melina and I bought many styrofoam balls at the dime store and covered them with strips of red and green gingham, braid, and ribbon. I thought they were just about the prettiest ornaments ever!

So in my family we have continued to make our own Christmas tree decorations through the years: cross-stitched sleighs, salt-dough stars, felt Santas and snowmen, silver balls with names spelled out in glitter, painted wooden figurines, and lacy paper snowflakes. Each year the decorations are different, but the tradition is to make them together.

An enjoyable way to involve children in the spirit of Christmas and in its festive preparation is in the making of homemade ornaments for the family tree. Perfect ornaments are not nearly as important as the sheer enjoyment of the activity of shared love. Here are some ideas:

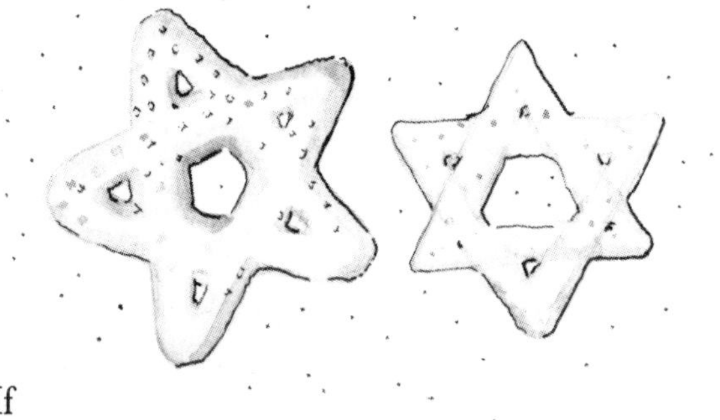

Salt-Dough Christmas Stars

4 cups flour (not self-rising)
1 cup salt
1 1/2 cups hot tap water

Mix and knead the dough until it is smooth and pliable. If it's too sticky, work in a little more flour. If the dough is too dry, moisten your fingers with water and knead a bit longer. Roll out the dough to about an inch thick and use cookie cutters in the shapes of stars, Santas, bells, angels, or whatever patterns you may have. Use your imagination to shape wreaths, candy canes, Christmas stockings, etc. (Even your children's Play Dough Fun Factory can be a good source for designs.) Push dough through a garlic press to make hair, moisten it and stick it on the ornament. With the point of a pencil, punch a hole for a string or tiny ribbon hanger to go through.

Right after cutting, bake at 350 degrees. (Tip: Keep an eye on the stars while baking; if air bubbles start to form, prick them with a needle.) When the dough becomes hard, it has finished baking. When cool, use acrylic paints to fill in the figures with color (or you can leave them unpainted for natural-colored ornaments). After they have dried completely, use a glossy or matte acrylic spray to apply the final finish.

A SECOND TREE FOR THE KIDS

In addition to the main tree in the living room, it's fun for kids to have a smaller tree to decorate themselves any way they choose. (You could trim off the top of the main tree and place it in a can of sand.) This will keep them busy making decorations — out of paper chains and glitter, snowflakes, or dolls — on days when it is too cold or rainy to play outside.

If you decide to have a second tree for the children, it can be as unique as their individual interests and personalities: a sports tree hung with baseball or football trading cards, a hobby tree covered with small paper airplanes colored with magic markers, a craft tree decorated with origami (Japanese paper-folding), a favorite toy tree featuring cuddly teddy bears, an art tree festooned with construction-paper cutouts and glitter stars, or a loved-one's tree highlighted with photos of family members set in homemade paper frames.

SNOWFLAKES

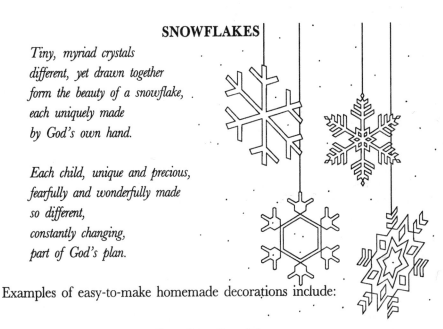

Tiny, myriad crystals
different, yet drawn together
form the beauty of a snowflake,
each uniquely made
by God's own hand.

Each child, unique and precious,
fearfully and wonderfully made
so different,
constantly changing,
part of God's plan.

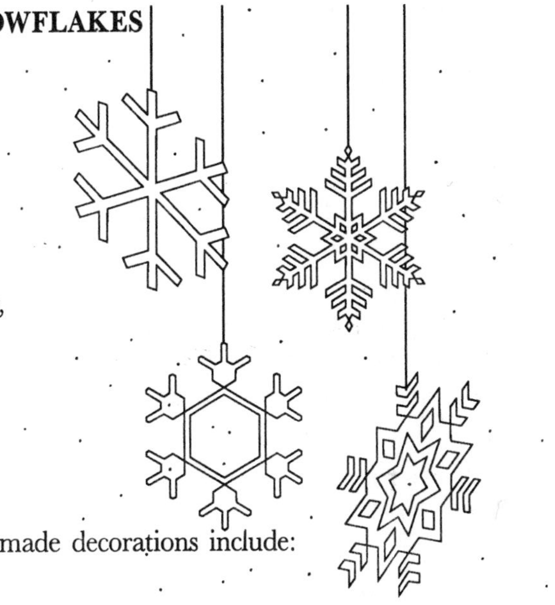

Examples of easy-to-make homemade decorations include:

Lacy Paper Snowflakes

For these, you will need several sheets of thin, white (silver, or gold) paper, a pair of sharp scissors, and some strong string. Fold a square of paper into eighths. Make random cuts in the paper, some curved and straight, some deep and shallow. You can add a dash of silver glitter to the edges.

Suspended on the branches of the children's tree by a string loop, these paper snowflakes add a homey, old-fashioned touch.

Paper Chains

Children also enjoy making paper chains, traditionally cut from red and green construction paper, to be used as decorations for the tree. As an interesting change, also try foil or wrapping paper. To make a different edge, use pinking shears to cut out the shapes. Children can decorate the chains with glitter. Join the links one to another with tape, white glue, or staples.

Paper Holiday Doll Chains

These can be made from red, green, or yellow paper, glittered white, silver, or gold. Brown wrapping paper adds a country Christmas touch. Fold the paper into an accordion that is just the width of your gingerbread man (or another favorite cookie-cutter pattern) and trace the doll shape on the front of the paper. Cut around it except for one area — the hands on each side. Unfold and hang!

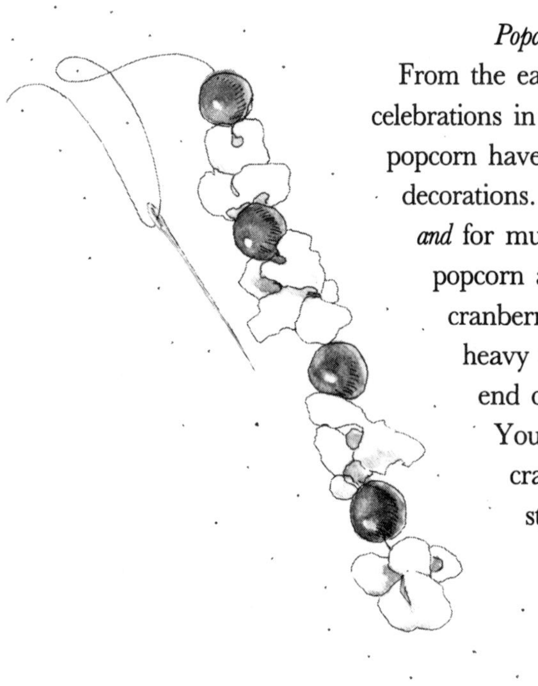

Popcorn and Cranberry Ropes

From the earliest days of Christmas celebrations in America, cranberries and popcorn have been part of the traditional decorations. Pop lots of corn for the ropes *and* for munching. Set out a big bowl of popcorn and a big bowl of fresh cranberries. Use a large needle and heavy thread. A button tied to the end of the string will be helpful. You can mix the popcorn and cranberries on the same chain or string them separately.

BABY SHOE ORNAMENTS

FIRST CHRISTMAS

Little infant, blue eyes wide
sits warmed beside
a Christmas fireside;
five stockings hang
above her head.
bright blue rocking horse,
red sequined Santa,
gingerbread boy gaze down
upon this new little one
only six weeks from her birth,
six short weeks
on the hectic moving ground;
arriving in time
to celebrate today
a special
Merry Christmas
with us,
Christmas love to stay.

To remind everyone of the special first Christmases of the babies in the family, every year you can hang baby shoes on the Christmas tree for each member of the household (sisters, brothers, Dad, Mom, and even grandparents). On the bottom of each shoe write the name and birth date of the family member.

PHOTO ORNAMENTS

Every year you can make a Christmas ornament with a current picture of each child. Take a metal lid from an orange juice can, spray it red, green or gold, and cut the photo to fit inside the "frame." Then poke a hole through the lid with an ice pick, string green crochet thread through the opening, and — *voila!* — a frame ornament.

TRAVEL MEMENTOS

Wherever we have traveled throughout the years, I have looked for ornaments which we could hang on the Christmas tree at home. One year I used a beautiful white sand dollar we had picked up on the beach in Georgia. I tied a thin velvet thread through it for a hanger and wrote on the back of it the year it was found and where it had come from. From Maine we brought back a small red wooden lobster to hang on the tree. From Colorado came miniature pine cones which I made into a small wreath ornament.

Such travel ornaments bring back a flood of memories of days gone by and places visited.

FAMILY MEMORY ORNAMENTS

One family we know makes their own hand-painted ornaments to preserve memories of family vacations, special recitals and awards, anniversaries, and graduations. Here's how to do it:

Cut thin plywood circles about three or four inches in diameter. Drill a tiny hole in the top of the circles for hangers to fit in.

First paint the front, back and sides with white acrylic paint. When the circles are fully dry, let the family artist sketch your memory picture on them. Paint the scenes with acrylics or fine-point markers. You can add trim around each circle and write the name of the event and date on the back. Use a small silver cord or red ribbon strung through the hole, hang and enjoy your family memories year after year!

SCENES OF CHRISTMAS PAST

Keepsakes add a homey, traditional touch to the home. Old family toys can be used to decorate the tree or the house.

In times past I have made decorations using our children's worn teddy bears, Alison's small porcelain dolls in their bright red and white dresses, our boys' old stuffed "Henry" dogs with fresh big bows wrapped around their necks and propped up in a chair — even an old tea set arranged near the Christmas tree or on a shelf.

You can also use a dollhouse, miniature cars and trucks on a shelf, your son's first train set or granddaughter's worn-out dolls, an antique quilt or old trunk to make a nostalgic scene beneath the tree.

Save your children's or grandchildren's wooden alphabet blocks they no longer play with. These are great for spelling out MERRY CHRISTMAS on the mantle or shelf or in front of dolls and bears.

One mother made life-sized Raggedy Andy dolls, dressed them in the embroidered suits she had handmade for her sons when they were just preschoolers, and set the stuffed pair near the Christmas tree seated in the old-fashioned child-sized rocking chairs the boys had used as toddlers. She also made infant dolls and dressed them in the baby clothes each of the youngsters had worn home from the hospital after their birth. A similar type of nostalgic display can be made using infant baptismal or christening gowns.

Stuffed teddy bears, geese and other stylized animals made from brightly colored swatches cut from children's baby blankets or grandmother's handmade quilts are also bright additions under the Christmas tree or beside the holiday fireplace.

"THESE ARE A FEW OF MY FAVORITE THINGS"

Collections of all types are a tradition in some families. In our home, we have a collection of Santas, some old and some new, which we get out and display every year at Christmas time. They include a Kris Kringle figure from Germany, a carved wooden Saint Nicholas from Taiwan, and a primitive American Santa Claus.

A collection of nutcrackers, Christmas plates, angels, ornaments, or Christmas bells — perhaps handed down through the generations — makes a bright, happy arrangement on a gaily decorated shelf or mantlepiece.

Collections — whether favorite dolls from childhood, old musical instruments decorated with red bows and sprigs of holly, or unique spoons from different places visited — can become very personal and traditional decorations.

SCENTS OF CHRISTMAS

My friend Gudbjorg remembers the wonderful aroma of orange peels simmering over the wood-burning stove in her childhood home in Norway. The warm, spicy citrus smell still brings back memories to her of snowy Norwegian Christmases.

Filling our homes with the scents of Christmas is a wonderful tradition. I boil cinnamon sticks and/or cloves in a pot filled with water, letting it simmer on the stove, uncovered, all day or all evening, continuing to add water as needed. To keep it fresher for a few days longer, you can keep the mixture in the refrigerator, covered, overnight.

Homemade Christmas Simmering Potpourri

Peels of 2 oranges
3 cinnamon sticks
12 whole cloves
2 1/2 cups water

Simmer on the stove. It will make your whole house smell festive and Christmasy.

In a pan of hot water you can also simmer evergreen sprigs or citrus peel and spices.

To add a holiday touch to each room, set out around the house lighted scented candles, decorative bowls or baskets of potpourri, fresh pine cones or leafy boughs of fragrant cedar or fir, a bowl of red and green apples, or a silver bowl of cranberries or pomander balls.

Pomander Balls

Making pomander balls is an old Christmas tradition dating back to the Victorian era. In my family we made so many of them when we were children that I am sure Mom must have thought, "Oh, dear, what will I do with another pomander ball?"

To make one of these aromatic balls, you will need an orange, a box of whole cloves, some powdered cinnamon, and a scrap of red or green ribbon. Choose a firm, fresh orange. Put down newspaper or a paper towel. Stick the points of the cloves into the orange, spacing them no farther than a half-inch apart. If the skin of the orange is too tough or too thick to penetrate, use the point of a large safety pin or a toothpick to prick holes for the cloves.

After you have dotted the whole surface of the orange with the cloves, shake it in a paper bag or roll on a paper plate of powdered cinnamon (a few tablespoons should be enough). This helps preserve the orange and adds to the spicy aroma.

Then let your pomander ball dry in a warm, airy place for a week or two (it will shrink a little) before tying a colorful holiday ribbon around it. You can put several of these balls in a silver bowl or basket, or place a piece of lacy fabric around the oranges, tie them with thin red velvet ribbons and give them as gifts.

A pomander ball is an enjoyable and inexpensive way to provide a fragrant scent to freshen a drawer, closet or small room.

You can also make a lovely Christmas ball by taking a styrofoam ball and decorating it by sticking into it tiny pine cones, cloves or bright dried flowers.

LET YOUR LIGHT SHINE

A traditional New England decoration is made by placing a single lighted candle in each window during the Advent season. On Christmas Eve the candles burn all night to light the way for the shepherds.

We brought this simple tradition back with us to Oklahoma from Maine. We use one electric candle to glow in each of our windows — our personal symbol that Jesus is the light of the world.

A FAMILY CHRISTMAS BANNER

Sharing a project like designing and putting together a simple Christmas banner to hang in your home is a good way to make a holiday memory. Get a large piece of felt or burlap and other different-colored squares of felt for letters and symbols. You'll also need some scissors and white glue.

Decide together on the symbols you'll portray on your banner — a lamb, crown, cross, manger, or star. You might also consider a dove and the word PEACE, or a star and the words JOY TO THE WORLD. Then make the banner together as a special holiday family undertaking.

FAMILY CHRISTMAS SCENES

DECEMBER EVENING

The warm family room glows
with balls checked red and green
upon a Christmas tree
and ornaments old and new,
angels, toys and stars,
felt Santas we made
and drummers red and blue;
the family room glows
with twinkle lights that burst with joy
and stockings hung under
a manger scene
and everywhere are satin bows
and candles set in spools of wood.

Baby sister sings and twirls nearby
and brothers draw what
their imaginations grow —
a space ship, elf or sledding scene,
mountains and pastures of green;
Mary and Joseph on Christmas night.
The sun has set; the night is cold
but inside all is warmth and light;
a table smells ready and hearts are glad
that Daddy's walking in.

It's fun to sit down at the kitchen table and let each person draw a scene from the Christmas story: shepherds on the hill seeing a bright host of angels, a manger scene with Mary and Joseph, or the arrival of the Wise Men and the shepherds.

You and your children may also enjoy the following family activities:

Christmas Acrostic

Let your children make up their own alphabet of Christmas — a simple Christmas acrostic:

A is for the *animals* in the stable.
B is for the *baby* who lay in the hay.
C is for the *cows* that grazed nearby
(or, our *Christmas* tree shining with lights).
D is for our *dinner* with turkey and trimmings.
E is for... (and so on through the alphabet)

Gingerbread House

Several years ago, Marianne, a mother of preschoolers, began a tradition of making gingerbread houses with her children. She puts the houses together and then gives the kids some tubes of icing and several bags of candy to use for decoration.

The houses are always colorful, and instead of eating them, the delighted youngsters save them from year to year (in the freezer) and are creating a gingerbread holiday village surrounded by cotton snow and tiny toy evergreen trees. (See the recipes and resources section for directions on how to make a gingerbread house.)

CHAPTER THREE

ACROSS THE MILES AND OTHER FAMILY SHARING TRADITIONS

Christmas wouldn't be the same
If we couldn't get in touch
With all the friends and family
Who mean so very much.

Anonymous

One of my favorite traditions at Christmastime is the writing and sending of our family newsletter. My main purpose is to communicate with loved ones and to share with them something of the year we have just experienced and God's faithful working in the midst of our joys, tears, and struggles, as well as the humorous happenings of our everyday lives. I also want to keep in touch with friends and family members far away, especially elderly ones who look forward to hearing about the growth of their great-granddaughter or great-grandnephew.

To me, one of the best things about writing newsletters is the family history that is slowly forming. I have a file of these "annual reports" and

I stick a copy of the new Christmas message in the file each year. I find it great fun to look back through the letters and see where we were and what we were doing at various times throughout the years past.

When my family and I were nearly two thousand miles away from home, I discovered that some of the best gifts at Christmas come in very small packages — envelopes — through the U.S. mail and bring the greatest joy. When in a strange place among unfamiliar people, it lifted our spirits and reminded us that somebody cared when we saw that friendly handwriting which brought news of family and friends back home. Pictures sent along with the Christmas letters brightened our refrigerator — and our lives.

"Oh, how Stuart has grown!" Alison exclaimed. "Wasn't Clint born just last summer? What night did we go to the hospital to see them? And look at Rachel and Molly — what cute red sailor dresses!"

Many people have dropped the habit of sending Christmas cards, thinking it a superfluous activity that takes too much time and expense. It does take time (next year I have got to start earlier!), and it does cost a bit — but oh, how exciting to hear about a close friend moving to Michigan, how encouraging to learn that a loved one is recovering from cancer, how thrilling to discover that another dear friend is expecting a baby, how interesting to read about how our friends in Algiers are spending Christmas. As Marjorie Holmes said, "What matters is they haven't forgotten us. They are reaching out to us across the miles and the years, sharing their joys and their sorrows, believing that we still care enough about them to want to know."[1]

Around Thanksgiving each year I usually begin thinking about the letter and asking Holmes and the kids for ideas: What do we want to include in our letter this time? What do you think are some of the special things that have happened this year? What are the highlights of these past twelve months?

If you are writing a Christmas newsletter, you can review the events of the year and let your children or teenagers add their *own* version of what has been the most important events in their lives since last Christmas.

Ellene, a veteran newsletter-writer, says that every December when she sets up the family Christmas tree, puts on some holiday music, and gets

---

[1]*Guideposts,* Dec. 1987, pp. 42,43.

cozy with a steaming mug of hot chocolate, an "inspirational moment" usually hits which helps her compose the annual letter.

CREATING THE FAMILY CHRISTMAS NEWSLETTER

Writing and sending a family Christmas newsletter is almost like having a little conversation with each friend and family member across the miles.

Here are some tips for putting together a family newsletter of your own:

- There are different ways to organize your material. You can do it month by month, highlighting the important happenings in each period, or you can keep a general record by the seasons of the year.

  Once the material is gathered, choose those items that would seem to be of most interest to your readers. Most of them (especially grandparents and great-grandparents) will want to know about the youngsters. When our kids were little, I wrote a short paragraph about each one of them.

  Let all the members of your family contribute thoughts and ideas — and humor. You may want to include a favorite Scripture verse or a personal note from each child, and have everyone sign the letter individually.

- You might type the letter in script (but it can also be handwritten or run off on a personal computer) and have one of the family artists decorate the borders. One year I used clip art (a candy cane and holly border) from the print shop because I was pressed for time.

- You can photocopy the letter on white, red, or green paper. Most office supply stores carry several types of decorative paper (both bond and computer) with seasonal themes and in a variety of colors and patterns.

- The letter doesn't have to be long. Some families send a Christmas postcard with a photocopied picture of the family on it or with some kind of art work or design added. This is inexpensive and provides a little room for a personal message.

Sometimes I condense my letter to one sheet, then reduce it on the photocopier to a half-sheet to better fit in with our Christmas cards. Often I write a personal note to each addressee at the bottom of the letter.

- The letter doesn't even have to arrive by December 25. You can do a New Year's family newsletter.

The important thing is not when or how well the annual newsletter is prepared and sent, just that it is done. Don't look upon it as an involved artistic or journalistic project, but simply as an enjoyable way of sharing news and greetings from your house to the homes of those who are most interested in what is happening with you and your family members.

CHRISTMAS TAPES

"Josh loved the Christmas story tape you sent!" my sister called to tell me. "He has listened to the stories several times and has taken the tape recorder to bed with him."

The idea originated one December when I was far away from beloved nieces and nephews for the holidays. I knew they would get piles of new toys, and that any little cards or gifts that I could send in the mail would soon get lost in the shuffle of discarded Christmas wrappings.

So I went to the children's department of our Yarmouth, Maine, library and spent some time with the librarian searching for some of the best Christmas stories available. We looked through several decades of books together and talked about some of our own childhood Christmas favorites.

I checked out "Baboushka," a Russian Christmas tale; a Tasha Tudor book of holiday stories; another book with legends of Christmas symbols (stories of how the poinsettia, tinsel, and pine tree became part of our holiday traditions); "The Fir Tree" by Hans Christian Andersen; "The Gift of the

Magi'' by O. Henry, and several others. Then, arms laden with stacks of books and story collections, I went out into the icy afternoon wind, warmed by the cheery thought of my idea.

I bought blank cassette tapes (five to a pack, inexpensive but good voice quality) and some white file folder labels. Back home again, I decorated the corners of the labels with drawings of holly sprigs and wrote on each one the name of the child for whom it was intended, the titles of the stories it contained, and the date of the recording. Then I taped my readings of the stories along with a few holiday poems, adding a little background music for the beginning and end — thus creating an individual holiday story tape appropriate for each age child. These were big hits among the children in our family!

(See the resources section at the back of this book for a list of stories you might want to include on your tape. The children's librarian in your local city, county, or church library is another valuable aid in helping you choose interesting, entertaining, inspirational, and educational stories geared to the age and interests of the child.)

Gift Idea

For a very personal Christmas (or birthday) gift, parents or grandparents can make a small library of tapes of the children's favorite stories, fairy tales or books which can be listened to all year long. These story tapes, in the parent's or grandparent's own voice, are often treasured by children, and are great ways to keep them entertained on long vacation trips, weekend jaunts, and even short errand hops around town. They are lifesavers for those days when the kids are sick in bed. They also help relieve boredom on rainy or cold days when they can't go outside and play. The tapes can be given alone, or the actual books can be included in the gift so the children can follow along with the readings ''all by themselves'' or aided by an adult or older brother or sister.

CASSETTE GREETINGS

There's nothing like greeting
Good friends, new and old,
To give holiday hours
All the warmth they can hold!
Anonymous

These warm holiday greetings can include the family singing Christmas songs, talking and sharing personal news items, reading a favorite Christmas story or poem (such as "The Night Before Christmas"), or perhaps a child playing his first carols on the piano or other musical instrument. With a current photo of children or family, these recorded messages make a nice way to keep in touch.

VIDEO GREETINGS

If you or a member of your family must be away from home during the holiday season, you can make a lively video "greeting card" to reach out and bring the family closer together in mind and heart, if not in miles.

In addition to the cassette tapes we sent to loved ones back home in Oklahoma, my family and I also borrowed a video camera from a friend and made a recorded Christmas greeting to share with them — complete with shots of our tree, a musical performance Alison and Chris were in at school, everyone talking (not all at once!), the sharing of tidbits of personal news, the singing of several Christmas favorites, and the sending of holiday wishes.

THE JOY OF CHRISTMAS CARDS

When Christmas cards begin arriving, put them in a brightly decorated or ribbon-bedecked basket on the dinner table. Each night as the family gathers for the evening meal, read one card aloud and pray for the family or friend who sent the holiday greeting. That way you can enjoy the cards and keep loved ones and friends in mind all through the month of December. Or you could read one card a week until they are all read, and do something kind (send a note, make a call, or drop off a gift of nut bread) for the person or family who sent it.

You can also hang the colorful cards on cords and make a bright, cheerful garland of them to stretch the length of the mantle, around the tree, or even across the room.

SHARING A CHRISTMAS CLASSIC

Life holds no sweeter thing than this:
To teach a little child the tale most loved on earth
And watch the wonder deepen in his eyes
There while you tell him of the Christ Child's birth;
The while you tell him of shepherds and a song,
Of gentle drowsy beast and fragrant hay
On which that starlit night in Bethlehem
God's tiny son and His young mother lay...[2]

Adelaide Love

At the beginning of the Advent season in December, favorite Christmas books and stories can be brought out and placed in a big basket tied up with a bright holiday bow and set by the Christmas tree to be enjoyed by all. Each year the family can also purchase a new Christmas book to add to the growing collection.

Every year we like to read aloud Leo Tolstoy's classic Christmas story, "Martin the Cobbler." One mother I know said that her favorite childhood Christmas memory was sitting on her dad's lap as he read "The Night Before Christmas." Another family reports that they always read the more recently popular children's books, *The Polar Express* and *A Cup of Christmas Tea.*

You can take turns reading by a crackling fireplace or around the holiday dinner table or Christmas tree. Other Christmas stories to read aloud after supper or before bedtime during the month of December include "The Gift of the Magi" by O. Henry, "Mr. Edwards Meets Santa Claus" by Laura Ingalls Wilder, and "The Legend of the Christmas Rose" by Selma Lagerlof.

Books and longer stories can be divided up and read in segments, such as one chapter a night. These include: *Raphael, The Herald Angel* by David Appel

---

[2]Used by permission of Heartland Samplers, 9947 Valley View Road, Eden Prairie, MN 55344.

and Merle Hudson, *The Story of the Other Wise Man* by Henry Van Dyke, "The Gifts of the Christ Child" by George MacDonald, *A Christmas Carol* by Charles Dickens, "A Christmas Dream and How It Came True" by Louisa May Alcott, and *The Best Christmas Pageant Ever* by Barbara Robinson.

(Check at your local library for collections of Christmas stories, both old and new, and start your own file of tales you love to read and listen to each year. See the resource list at the end of this book for other suggestions.)

CLASSIC CHRISTMAS MOVIES

Have an "un-stress night": gather the family together, get a take-out or call-in pizza, snuggle up in sleeping bags with plenty of popcorn and cider, and watch some classic Christmas movies or holiday specials on television. Our favorite old Christmas movies are *It's a Wonderful Life* and *Miracle on 34th Street.*

A new tradition you would like to start from this section:

CHAPTER FOUR

JOY IN THE MAKING: GIFTS FOR CHILDREN (AND GROWN-UPS) TO CREATE

The best gifts are tied with heartstrings.

Anonymous

When children have an opportunity to make presents, they get to use their natural energy and creativity, and experience the joy of giving. Gifts kids create are presents from the heart and are treasured down through the years. I remember the fun my sisters and I had making a huge Christmas tablecloth for Mom's big dining table. We got red net fabric from the sewing shop and spent hours cutting and sewing sequins on felt trees, bells, stars, and elves to go around the colorful tapestry — we thought it was wonderful!

Pick a Saturday before Christmas and gather with a friend (or friends) and children to make thoughtful gifts such as:

Gourmet Bean Soup Mix

The mix is made up of five different beans sealed in a zip-lock bag, with a stiff paper label stapled over and decorated, and the recipe written on the back.

Ingredients in the zip-lock bag include: 1/2 cup each of split green peas, lentils, baby limas, black turtle beans, and pinto beans.

Recipe: Soak the beans overnight. In an 8-quart Dutch oven, combine beans with 2 tablespoons chopped parsley, 1 bay leaf, 3/4 teaspoon each of marjoram and thyme. Add 10 cups of chicken or ham stock. Bring to a boil, and skim off the foam. Reduce heat. Simmer 2 1/2 hours or until the beans are tender.

In a skillet, saute 1 chopped onion, 4 chopped carrots, 3 chopped celery ribs, 2 cloves of minced garlic in 1/2 cup of butter. Then stir the sauteed vegetables into the beans and stock. Add 1/2 lb. cubed ham, 1 28-ounce can of cut-up tomatoes, 1 tablespoon prepared mustard, and salt and pepper to taste. Simmer and enjoy!

Whole Wheat Pancake Mix

In a bowl, mix 1 cup unbleached flour, 1 cup whole wheat flour, 2 tablespoons sugar, 1 tablespoon baking powder, 1/2 teaspoon salt, and place the mixture in a zip-lock bag. Write the recipe on the label, decorate it, and staple it to the bag:

Recipe: Add 1 3/4 cup milk
2 eggs, beaten
2 tablespoons vegetable oil
to the dry ingredients and mix lightly.
Makes 4-6 servings of great pancakes!

Spicy Cinnamon Sticks

A bunch of extra-long cinnamon sticks tied with red- or green-plaid ribbons and a sprig of holly or baby's breath makes a festive, spicy gift for a favorite person's room.

Favorite Teacher's Gifts

Melt chocolate in the microwave and pour into plastic Christmas tree molds with a stick inserted to make solid milk chocolate suckers. Cover with a tiny plastic sack and decorate with red or green curly ribbon.

Painted Wooden Ornaments

Pre-cut wooden Santas, candy canes, or other holiday shapes you can pick up at a hobby shop are hand-painted with bright acrylics and finished with a matte spray lacquer. The child's name and age are written on the back as a special memento. A hanger or gold thread can be added for use on the tree. Or a pin can be glued on the back to make a Christmas pin to wear on a coat or sweater.

Cookie Cutter Ornaments

Take a metal gingerbread man (or tree, house, star or other shape) cookie cutter. Glue stiff Christmas ribbon or felt to the back. Tie a bright ribbon through the top and you have a shiny ornament for the tree that's easy enough for a preschooler to make.

Hand-Painted Wall Hangings

Cut a length of any color burlap and pour some bright acrylic paint into aluminum pie tins. Have each child put his handprint across the top of the burlap. You can paint below the print the youngster's name and the year. The following verse can also be painted below the handprint:

Although we are sorta small
And leave our fingerprints on the wall,
This will help you remember the way
Our handprints looked on Christmas Day.

Put a thin dowel rod across the top of the yarn as a hanger. Fringe the bottom, and you have a memorable gift for grandparents or favorite aunt and uncle.

Handprint T-Shirts

You can also get a white sweatshirt or T-shirt for Grandma or Granddad and do the handprinting as explained above with little hearts around each child's print, name, and date or age. (A red T-shirt with white handprints makes a delightful alternative.)

"My Very Own Book"

A wonderful gift for a child to make and give — especially to parents or grandparents — is an original book.

Your youngster can make up a story, relate a true personal experience, or write his own rendition of a favorite anecdote or familiar fairy tale. The Christmas story retold in your child's own words and illustrated by him would be a treasured gift. He can also create a book about a favorite hobby or interest — animals, sports, or space. A book can be made about his family history or about his hopes and dreams of what he would like to do or become someday.

Once the youngster has come up with his story idea, help him write it out on scratch paper. Then it can be revised, with any necessary changes made on the practice copy.

Next, help him copy the story on good white paper, leaving room for pictures if the book is to be illustrated. (Crayons or water-based markers work well for this purpose.)

To make a cover for the book, use colored construction paper stapled evenly around the edge of the pages. A cover can also be made out of cardboard sealed with contact paper. Holes are then punched on each page at the top, middle, and bottom of the left margin, and the pages are bound together by threading yarn or ribbon through the holes and tying them together.

(If you prefer, you can order hardback blank books with a white cover — ready for illustration — for your child to use to make his book. See the resource list for the address of Sundance Publishers and Treetop Publishing who provide these materials.)

These special books, created by the children themselves, become treasured keepsakes. Youngsters can express their love and appreciation for family and friends by creating and giving them a wonderful addition to their libraries. Books — especially those made by beloved children and grandchildren — are gifts that can be enjoyed again and again!

Other Handmade Gift Ideas

- Get a Christmas mug and inside it put homemade spiced tea in a plastic baggie or hot chocolate mix wrapped in red or green tissue. Tie a bow around the baggie or tissue and put in a Santa cinnamon stick (see illustration below):

- Tri-Bead Ornaments: With proper supervision, even a two-year-old can make these bright holiday ornaments. You can purchase tri-beads at almost any hobby shop. String them on a pipe cleaner, and then bend it into the shape of a candy cane or wreath. Tie a bow at the top and slip a wire hanger through the center of the bow. Tie another red bow around the candy cane. These ornaments glisten and shine on the tree when the Christmas lights are turned on.

- Rudolph, the Red-Nosed Candy Cane: Take a twelve-inch pipe cleaner and cut it in half. Then cut one of the six-inch cleaners in half. Wrap the other six-inch cleaner around the end of a medium-sized candy cane. Then twist the shorter pipe cleaners around and bend to look like

antlers. With white glue, put on two small (7 mm) wiggle eyes and a tiny red pompom nose — and, presto! You have Rudolph, the Red-Nosed Candy Cane! This makes a nice surprise for a favorite teacher, close friend at school, or for use as a special package decoration.

- Old-fashioned potholder: With a loom and bright-colored loops, children can create pretty potholders (and also stay busy on those cold, rainy or snowy days before Christmas).

Handmade Wrapping Paper

Many children enjoy wrapping the gifts they have made, and even designing their own wrapping paper. Here are some ideas:

- Glittery gift wrap: All you need is some brightly colored tissue paper, adhesive spray, and gold, silver or green glitter. Unfold the tissue and smooth it out, spray it with adhesive, and then sprinkle on the glitter. Let dry before wrapping.

- Stamp pattern gift wrap: Get some stamps (Teddy bears, Santas, rocking horses, Christmas scenes, candy canes, etc.) and a red or green ink pad. Let your child decorate plain white wrapping paper with colorful stamp patterns. Add a red or green curly ribbon.

Even preschoolers can enjoy this simple craft, and it gives them an opportunity to be involved in the exciting preparation of gifts.

- Handprint gift wrap: For your child's own handprint paper, you will need: 1) white shelf paper or brown wrapping paper, 2) red acrylic or tempera paint in a small dish or aluminum pie pan, and 3) an old shirt or apron.

Before beginning to make this unique Christmas wrapping paper, dress the child in the old shirt or apron. Cover the floor or table with several layers of newspapers or a vinyl dropcloth — to avoid spills in the wrong places!

Working with one color at a time, unroll the paper and allow the child to dip his hand into a dish of paint and then press down firmly on the paper (with his fingers spread apart). Then he can put his hand in again and repeat the action — leaving space for other color prints. After half of the paper has been done in red, let the child wash his hands and begin with green (or another color).

This is an enjoyable rainy or snowy day activity and makes a bright wrapping paper that Grandma or Grandpa will cherish for years to come.

Family History Gifts

Older children and teens can interview grandparents or older family members (perhaps at Thanksgiving or during summer vacation) and then tape record, write or type the stories and make them into little cassette albums or books. These make a perfect gift of family history to send out to cousins and extended family. A family tree can be added. Or a collection of "Grandma's Favorite Recipes" can benefit the whole family and later generations.

MORE FAMILY GIFTS TO MAKE

A Gift of Memories:
Strengthening the Ties That Bind

You can create cherished gifts, stir up remembrances of times gone by, and strengthen family ties by making and giving a gift of memories.

Here are some ideas:

- A family collection of recipes: One Christmas after our mother died, my sister Georgia handwrote many of Mom's favorite recipes (those handed down to her), and then copied and bound them together with a golden cord. For the collection you could also have everyone contribute favorite recipes and old ones passed down through the family.

- Frame your child's special colorful drawing for Grandma or Granddad. Or you could frame a fifty-year-old doily your grandmother crocheted, an old quilt square, or a cross-stitch sampler. You could restore an old family photograph, tintype or painting, or frame an important family document.

- "This Is Your life": One of my most cherished gifts from my mother is a red photo album filled with pictures from my childhood to the present. One autumn Mom spent hours separating stacks of photos of the six of us siblings — pictures of our growing-up years; our grandparents, aunts, etc. — and presented a "This Is Your Life" album to each of us children with a note she had written in the front cover at Christmas time.

- A gift of family history: Make a video taped oral history of a grandparent, great-aunt or -uncle, and give copies at Christmas. Create an imaginative video tape of old slides and family pictures and set it to music.

- Write a book about your family. Your family history book can include stories about a great-grandfather who first immigrated to the United States or who was in the Civil War, along with tales of other notable family members, copies of important documents, and other items of historical interest to the family. What a treasure!

One grandmother transforms favorite family stories (including humorous adventures) into picture books which she writes and illustrates for the children in the clan.

I am making a book of stories about my mother with little recollections from different members of the family — including some poems Mom wrote and her favorite scriptures and sayings. I hope to finish it *someday!*

- Start a family newsletter to help keep extended family, military members, and college kids in different parts of the country connected. The first edition can be the Christmas or New Year's edition. It can be handwritten, typed and copied, or computer-generated, and can include everything from news of the family to anecdotes from the past.

The best way to gather information is to write a relative and say something like: "I'm planning to start a family newsletter, but in order for us to stay in touch, I need *your* news. Please send me any information — travels, honors, moves, new births — anything you would like to share about yourself and your family. I'll put it together and send it out."

Keeping the family newsletter going shouldn't fall on only one person's shoulders. Have someone be the "Information Center" who keeps up on addresses and the latest news. One or two members can write the newsletter, while another takes care of mailing it.

As your newsletter continues, it could have headings or columns such as:

- Three Cheers for You! (Achievements, graduations, etc.)

- Wedding Bells (Engagements and upcoming nuptials)

- Welcome to the Family! (Birth and adoption announcements)

- Notable News (Interesting trips, promotions, career changes, military service)

- I Remember When (Anecdotes about the "good old days")

- Upcoming Birthdays and Anniversaries

- New Addresses and Corrections

At the bottom of the newsletter's last page, you could have a tear-off-and-mail section with an RSVP for the next family reunion or gathering.[1]

> Although these gifts may not be expensive, they will be cherished and your efforts will be both worthwhile and appreciated as you give the precious gift of memories.

GRATITUDE IS THE MEMORY OF THE HEART: Writing thank you notes and letters after Christmas is a wonderful tradition for a family to start. Give your child a box of colorful thank you notes and stamps to use to express appreciation to grandparents, aunts and uncles, or friends for gifts received at Christmas. As you write notes of appreciation for people's thoughtfulness, your child can follow suit.

A Gift of Time

Each family member gives a coupon to the others with a promised service (like cleaning, vacuuming, snow shoveling) or time spent together (like a day at the museum with Dad or the zoo with Mom, etc.). It might read, "This coupon entitles you to breakfast in bed any Saturday of your choice in the month of January. Love, Jennie." These can be written on blank index cards,

[1]The above was excerpted from my article, "Drawing a Family Circle," which appeared in the March 1991 issue of *Focus on the Family*.

wrapped, or put in envelopes and placed in Christmas stockings or hung on the tree.

The Gift of Teaching

Helping someone you love learn something new is a good way to show love at Christmas.

One dad gave his teenage son lessons in computer programming. A mom gave her daughter sewing lessons one Christmas. In both these cases, the parent and the child shared the fun of learning something together, but the young people also learned a skill to enrich their lives.

The Gift of Listening

This gift is tough to give if we are rushed or used to listening only half-heartedly. But one of the best gifts we can give a child, spouse, or family member is that of a truly open ear, mind, and heart. And Christmas can be a wonderful time to begin, as we listen attentively while they share their stories: their hopes, their frustrations, and their dreams.

CHAPTER FIVE

TRADITIONS OF HOSPITALITY

Our house is open, Lord, to thee;
Come in, and share our Christmas tree!
We've made each nook and corner bright,
Burnished with yellow candle-light.

But light that never burns away
Is only thine, Lord Jesus, Stay,
Shine on us now, our Christmas Cheer —
Fill with thy flame our whole New Year![1]

Luci Shaw

One of the best parts of the Christmas season is inviting friends — young and old — into our homes to share a cup of Christmas tea and some holiday cookies, to visit with neighbors we rarely see during normal hectic school and work weeks, to have

[1]From a greeting card published by World Wide Publications — a ministry of the Billy Graham Evangelistic Association, 1303 Hennepin Avenue, Minneapolis, Minnesota 55403.

extended family over for a potluck dinner, or to host a small group of children for a "make it and take it" craft party.

In whatever form, traditions of hospitality are special expressions of Christmas love you can find in your own backyard, family room, or neighborhood. Christmas gatherings don't have to be large or elaborate — hot cherry pie and coffee, a favorite desert from your kitchen, or even "storebought" gingerbread men or cookies, can form the backdrop for a memorable evening.

Here are some of my favorite Christmas hospitality traditions:

NEIGHBORHOOD COOKIE EXCHANGE

A neighborhood cookie exchange is a great idea for a winter block party. It's also a good way to get neighbors together for a short time to fellowship and chat in a busy season during which they might otherwise only catch a glimpse of each other pulling in and out of their driveways.

Two families who serve as "hosts" can make invitations on a sheet of white paper. Then they can have the paper copied on bright red or green card stock, which the kids can cut out, decorate with crayons or stickers, and hand deliver.

Each family brings a batch of two dozen homemade cookies (their own specialities) which they can use to swap. That way everyone goes home with a variety of different and interesting cookies. Punch, cookie-tasting, and caroling follow.

The cookie exchange can be turned into a service project (and also save some unneeded calories) by having small gift sacks set out on the table. Guests fill the sacks with different cookies, tie them with curly red or green ribbons, and then all go together to the local nursing home to deliver them to senior citizens!

FESTIVAL OF THE COOKIES AND CRECHE

On a holiday evening, members of a church, neighbors or friends gather together. Each family brings their favorite cookies with the recipe (photocopied for all present) and their family creche (nativity set). After enjoying the cookies and cider, during a time of sharing, each family tells about their nativity set: where it came from, how they got it, and any special significance or strong sentiments attached to it. This is a wonderful way to get to know one another better.

INTERNATIONAL FLAIR

Invite an international student from a local college or university to spend Christmas with your family, or to spend a weekend in your home during the holiday season. The student gets to learn first-hand about American customs (and doesn't have to be alone in the dormitory for the holidays, as so many are). You and your children also benefit from learning about the student's nation, life, and culture.

Our friends, Penny and Richard Hook, made a tablecloth which they use when international guests come to share holiday meals. They sketch each guest's handprint on the tablecloth. Afterwards, Penny sews around the handprint in bright embroidery thread and stitches the student's name and country beside it. The "international tablecloth" is brought out and enjoyed each Christmas, a record of foreign guests whom the family has entertained and shared the joy of Christmas with through the years.

ONE IS SILVER, AND THE OTHER GOLD

The road is never long
when going to the home of a friend.
Anonymous

As the old Girl Scout song says: "Make new friends/ and keep the old,/ one is silver,/ and the other gold." Soon after Thanksgiving, my family and I decide on several people — both new friends (silver) and old friends (gold) — we want to have over for dinner individually or as a family group some time during the month of December. We invite them well in advance and mark the date of their arrival on our calendar. (I find that if we don't plan ahead, things can get so hectic there is no time left for hospitality.)

After a shared meal, warm conversation by the fireplace, and perhaps some games, we take this person's or family's picture in front of the hearth. Afterwards, we place the picture in our Christmas photo album and send a duplicate to them.

REACH OUT TO OTHERS

Involve your neighbors, especially newcomers — young and old — in your Christmas celebration.

1. Have a birthday party for Jesus for the children in your neighborhood. This helps youngsters understand and celebrate the real meaning of Christmas and can be given any time during the holiday season (even between Christmas and New Year's.) Serve a birthday cake for Jesus with one big candle in the middle or with big candle numbers for the current year.

For a gift for Jesus, have each guest bring a canned good or toy for a needy child. Sing Christmas songs, read a special holiday story, or let guests act out the nativity story with the props you supply.

2. Go caroling together. Hand out invitations door to door at least a week ahead, meet at a home (with your destination — nursing homes, residences of shut-ins, or other neighborhood areas— already mapped out), provide song sheets for carolers, and enjoy the outing!

3. Be caring toward newcomers in your neighborhood or church. People who have recently moved feel especially lonely during the holidays. Because they have left behind familiar surroundings and activities, friends, and family, they are often not invited to Christmas events. It means so much to be included in the holiday festivities of their new area. You can help build a bridge of friendship by:

- Organizing a block potluck supper or cookie exchange

• Taking the new family a plant in a basket, a loaf of nut bread, or a plate of cookies

• Inviting a new neighbor to your church's Christmas Eve service or a community holiday event

• Calling and asking to pick up a newcomer couple for a Sunday school party (they might be reluctant to come alone or not know how to get to the unfamiliar residence)

CHRISTMAS CAROLING PARTY

The weekend before Christmas, it's fun to invite a few singles and families, including all the children, for a light potluck supper (or just for cheese and crackers, fruit, tiny sandwiches and chips, and various other treats). With this great group of mixed ages, you can snack, visit, play games, and then go out caroling together in the neighborhood.

NEIGHBORHOOD CHRISTMAS COFFEE

Each Christmas we share
With friends both far and near
Makes our years together
So memorable and dear.
Anonymous

One year a few weeks before Christmas when we had just moved to Oklahoma City with three little ones under five and no family or friends in the area, I was feeling quite isolated and blue. All three of the children had just come through a bout with bronchitis, and cabin fever had set in. I'll never forget my excitement when another mom, Elaine, brought around to each door special invitations to her "neighborhood Christmas coffee." As a newcomer, it was the highlight of my first holiday season in a strange new environment!

The neighborhood get-together was held on the next Saturday. Each person brought a coffee ring or a loaf of nut bread and Elaine served tea, coffee, and hot cider. The warmth and friendliness I experienced was one of the best Christmas gifts I received that year. I got to meet all the neighbors on the block, including some other moms with small children, and soon afterwards we began a playgroup with our children.

HOSPITALITY TO THE CHILDREN IN YOUR LIFE

When school lets out for the holidays, it's time to make memories and have some fun in the kitchen, playroom or den. Here are some good ideas for keeping youngsters entertained during the Christmas season by involving them in the holiday festivities.

Kids' Cooking Party

A kids' cooking party is an excellent way to show hospitality to the children in your life (including yours, those of close friends, grandchildren, or a few of the youngsters on your block)! You can invite an assortment of kids to come over for an afternoon of cooking, tasting and decorating gingerbread boys and girls (which you have already made or bought) using raisins, colored icing, red hots (tiny spicy cinnamon candy) or M&Ms. They can take home some of the cookies to share.

Or if you're really brave and jolly, you can have each guest don an apron and cook up a storm! You should have all the ingredients ready to make one gigantic pizza or a bunch of individual pizza pies. Your youthful guests can decorate a giant chocolate chip cookie or make a "Star of Bethlehem." (See the recipe section in the back of the book). Your junior cooks can also create special Christmas treats for the birds.

Bird treat: First roll a pine cone in a mixture of peanut butter and honey and then in a pie tin filled with bird seed. A mixture of suet and bird seed can also be used. Tie on a thread or thin wire for a hanger and let each child take home his feeder to hang outside on a tree branch. In winter, food sources for birds are often depleted, so remembering to care for our feathered friends at Christmas time is not only a very old and enduring tradition, it is also a good way to demonstrate God's love and concern for "all creatures great and small."

"Make It and Take It" Craft Party

Christmas vacation is a good time to invite children in for a "make it and take it" craft party. You supply the materials and they make a few gifts and ornaments. (There are lots of ideas in the previous chapter, "Joy in the Making," for gifts kids can make.)

Your young guests can also make stained-glass cookies (see the recipes section), Santa apples or holiday cones.

Santa Apples

Every year in the Neeley home, "Santa apples" (for looking, not eating) are made just the way their grandmother used to prepare them years ago. Here are the necessary ingredients:

- 1 upside-down apple (shined with Crisco) for Santa's body
- 3 or 4 cranberries on toothpicks for his legs and arms (allow the arms to angle in a slight "V" and the legs to come a bit forward)
- 1 toothpick to be used in the back as a prop to help the pudgy old elf stand up
- 1 large marshmallow for the head
- cranberries for his red hat
- several fresh cloves for his eyes and mouth and the buttons down the front of his coat
- a ball of cotton attached with glue (and coming to a point) for a beard

Holiday Cones

We used to make these for birthday parties, but they are delicious and fun to make and eat at Christmas. You will need:

- 1 regular-sized box of cake mix (your favorite flavor) and any ingredients the mix requires
- 24 flat-bottomed ice cream cones
- frosting (and sprinkles, if desired for decoration)

Directions: Prepare the cake mix by following the instructions on the box. Spoon cake batter into each cone until it is half full, and then place the cones on a baking sheet or in a muffin tin. Bake for 30 minutes at 350 degrees. Cool before frosting. Sprinkle red or green sugar crystals on the top. You can decorate them to look like Frosty the Snowman or Santa.

Frosty: Use white frosting and white coconut for his body, black licorice for his hat, and red candies for his eyes and mouth.

Santa: Spread frosting on top of the cupcakes. Then add coconut for a beard and the fur of the hat (mini-marshmallows can also be used for white), chocolate chips or raisins for eyes, and red hots (cinnamon candies) for a mouth and hat.

"Grown-Up" Mother-Daughter Christmas Tea Party

The little girls in your life will enjoy dressing up in their prettiest party dresses and coming over for a "grown-up" tea party. (Moms, Grandmoms, and Teddy bears are invited too, of course!) You can bring out the china dishes or Christmas plates and serve miniature muffins, tea cakes, or gaily decorated cookies along with apple cider in dainty tea cups.

(There are lots of other ideas for entertaining children and adults in the section about the joy of making gifts and in the tree-trimming and ornaments section.)

CHAPTER SIX

TRADITIONS OF SERVICE

The Joy of Giving
Somehow not only for Christmas
But all the long year through,
The joy that you give to others
Is the joy that comes back to you.
And the more you spend in blessing
The poor and lonely and sad,
The more of your heart's possessing
Returns to make you glad.

John Greenleaf Whittier

Giving and serving together as a family brings us closer and helps us appreciate the true meaning of Christmas. Making service a traditional part of our holidays leaves a special memory with our children as they grow, and hopefully helps us all discover ways to serve throughout the year.

FOOD BASKET TRADITION

In the fall, a small basket is placed on the dining room table, and everyone in the family — including the children — is encouraged to do little odd jobs to earn some extra money. Each family member contributes something, no matter how small. Just before Christmas, parents and children go to the grocery store together to select items for a lovely holiday food basket to be presented to a less fortunate family in the community.

VOLUNTEER SERVICE WORK

One way to make Christmas not only more meaningful for the family, but also more enjoyable for others, is by doing volunteer service work. You and your family might want to band together to work a shift serving a meal at a soup kitchen at the Salvation Army center or in a city or church rescue mission.

ADOPT-A-FAMILY TRADITION

The Mayer family "adopted" a single young mom with three small children in the Chicago area for Christmas. The Mayers received the family member's names from a community agency which supplied them with pictures of the children and a list of their ages and particular needs. They went out to spend one afternoon during the busy Christmas season shopping for food, gifts, and toys. Then they went home and wrapped everything in bright holiday paper, ribbons, and bows, and included a card and a photo of themselves before delivery to the needy family.

SALVATION ARMY GIFT-WISH TREE

Another means of assuring a very merry Christmas for a needy boy or girl in your community is provided by the Salvation Army. In cooperation with local merchants, businesses, and civic groups, this caring agency collects the Christmas wishes of area underprivileged children and hangs the lists on a special tree, often in a popular shopping mall or center. Then interested individuals and families can select a particular child's list (which usually includes his or her first name, plus sizes and descriptions of the items needed or desired), buy the gifts, and return them to the store or the Salvation Army which will see that they reach the child by Christmas.

This is a wonderful way to share in the joy of giving while shedding the light of Christmas cheer to a deserving youngster. It also serves to remind us that "inasmuch as we have done it unto one of the least of these," His young brothers and sisters, we have done it unto the Christ Child Himself!

PROJECT ANGEL TREE

In a similar way, Project Angel Tree sets up Christmas trees in community centers, hospitals or churches and hangs on them the names of children of prison inmates. Project Angel Tree is an outreach of Prison Fellowship Ministries which distributes Christmas presents (toys and much-needed clothing) to children all over the United States who would otherwise be forgotten. For more information write:

Angel Tree
P.O. Box 17500
Washington, D.C. 20041
or phone 1-800-762-2551

GIVING IN SECRET

One family has an interesting tradition of giving. Each Christmas they look around to see whom they might give to that year. Once they have selected the person, they set aside a portion of their family Christmas resources to make an *anonymous* contribution to that needy person's holiday cheer.

One year they noticed an older woman in town who lived on a fixed income. They watched her to see what she might need, and decided on a beautiful, warm sweater. Their joy was extended as they saw her wear that sweater day in and day out during the long, cold winter.

Another year they spotted a little girl from a family in their church and realized that they had never seen her in a dress. They picked out a lovely dress with shoes to match, which they wrapped and sent anonymously. Every Sunday thereafter that little girl wore that pretty dress and shoes to church.

The parents of this generous family enjoy this tradition a great deal, but it has become their boys' favorite part of the Christmas season.

MORE GOOD WAYS TO SERVE OTHERS

There are always creative ideas for service when we look for them.

One year it may be helping collect gloves, hats, and scarves for a shelter for the homeless in our city. Another year it may be taking donations of blankets and coats or paying the electric bill for a family who otherwise would have a dark and cold Christmas.

There are also such worthwhile organizations as Toys for Tots and Meals on Wheels which serve the very young and the elderly and infirm. Many churches, especially those in downtown areas, need volunteer workers to provide or serve daily meals to hungry street people.

(For other opportunities of service at Christmas time, check with your church or other religious, social, and civic agency in your area.)

One idea might be to send a package of gifts to a missionary, elderly shut-in, or overseas serviceperson. Even such seemingly insignificant services as caroling at a nursing home can be occasions of great joy and blessing for all concerned. Instead of giving your own holiday party, for example, consider hosting one for foster children or youngsters in a children's hospital, orphanage, or a shelter for homeless families.

SPONSOR A CHILD

One of the best ways to extend the joy of Christmas giving throughout the year, and make a real difference in the life of a child, is by sponsoring a needy boy or girl somewhere in the United States or world through an organization like COMPASSION INTERNATIONAL, WORLD VISION, FEED THE CHILDREN, UNICEF, CHRISTIAN CHILDREN'S FUND or other childcare programs. For around twenty dollars a month, you can provide food, clothing, medical care, and educational opportunities for a needy child. Best of all, you can also help *provide hope and help all year through.*

Christmas is a great time to start a family tradition of fostering "peace on earth, good will to men," by helping needy children of all ages, religions, races, and nationalities — both at home and throughout the world. It is a tradition that will bring joy and cheer all year long.

(See the resources list at the end of this book for the names and addresses of several reputable, deserving childcare agencies.)

CHAPTER SEVEN

CHRISTMAS EVE AND CHRISTMAS DAY TRADITIONS

May the child who lives with us
Gently teach us how to find
Joy and trust in one another —
Lasting faith in all mankind.

Anonymous

The centerpiece of Christmas Eve at our house is the candlelight service which is held by the decorated tree or festive fireplace. The only light in the room is from a few well-placed candles.

Beforehand, we divide up among the children the Christmas story as recounted in the second chapter of the book of Luke. (One Christmas Eve, five-year-old Alison was just a beginning reader, but she wanted to take part so she memorized her portion.) Each child reads his or her segment of the story in sequence. Then we join in a few carols together, accompanied by the guitar or piano — or *a cappella.*

Afterwards we may have a time of sharing: a humorous family story, what we are especially thankful for this year, or our most memorable Christmas.

For the last song of the evening, each person holds a white candle with a small round cardboard base. With all the lights out, except our tiny candles, we quietly sing "Silent Night." Then after a short time of prayer, each family member gets to pick one gift from under the tree and open it.

We began this special candlelight service tradition when the kids were too young to stay up to go to church late at night. Once the excitement of gift opening had died down, they were sent to bed, while my husband and I stayed up to see that Santa got the stockings well filled. Now that the children are older we continue the candlelight tradition, although we also attend the midnight worship service.

IS THERE ROOM IN YOUR INN?

The Snowbarger family puts up a manger scene early in December, but without the Baby Jesus in it. At bedtime on Christmas Eve, all the lights are turned out and everyone holds a little candle. Daddy is the innkeeper. Mom and the four boys go around to the bedroom doors (while Daddy moves quickly from room to room), knocking and asking, "Is there room in your inn?" Repeatedly the answer comes back: "No, no room here." Finally the children get to the living room where the innkeeper answers, "Yes, there's room here!" They all go in, place Baby Jesus in the manger, bow down, and sing, "O come, let us adore Him."

Instead of hanging stockings on the mantelpiece, this family follows the quaint Mexican tradition of putting out their shoes by the bedroom door, filled with straw. The Wise Men's camels come by during the night, eat the straw, and then fill the empty shoes with candy for the little ones.

ACT OUT THE NATIVITY

One of my favorite memories is when Alison crawled in the room as a lamb (a large piece of white fake fur draped convincingly over her body) with Chris beside her as a shepherd (dressed in a housecoat for a robe and carrying a hockey stick for a staff) as he told us his version of the first Christmas.

Another time Alison dressed up as Mary and carried a doll wrapped in a blanket as she shared the Christmas story.

With a minimum of parental guidance and supervision and a maximum of inspiration and imagination — broomsticks or yardsticks for staffs, bathrobes or old sheets for shepherds' garments, hand towels for makeshift turbans — the young people in the family can put on their own Christmas pageant. You can provide the necessary props, such as: foil to make a halo, a white sheet for the angel Gabriel, a shawl for Mary, a doll for Baby Jesus, homemade glitter gowns for the Wise Men, etc.

With these handmade costumes and props (and aided by friends and cousins), the children can act out the Christmas story as part of your annual Christmas Eve celebration.

Often this "do-it-yourself" version is more fun — and also more meaningful and memorable — than the most elaborate and polished of adult-staged productions.

A PUZZLE FOR CHRISTMAS EVE

On Christmas Eve a new giant puzzle is put out in the family room. Between then and New Year's, family members (and friends and relatives who drop by) can work on putting the pieces together. The goal is to have the whole picture completed by New Year's Day.

As visitors come and go throughout the holiday season, the puzzle table provides a good place to gather, chat, snack, and enjoy each other's company as you keep your hands busy working on a family project.

GIVE BABY JESUS A GIFT OF YOURSELF

. . . only know love
for the young child, Christ,
straight and wise.
Carl Sandburg

Legend and song tell us that the Little Drummer Boy gave all he had to the Christ Child — he played music for Him upon his drum. You and your family can make a Christmas Eve tradition based on this same principle.

On a construction paper star, name tag, or other ornamental piece of paper, each member of the family writes what he will give of himself to the Baby Jesus this Christmas. These "gifts" may range from a promise to "be nicer to brother," to reading through the Bible during the coming year, to a commitment to work on an area of life that needs special attention — even a vow to complete an important assignment or project or to sacrifice a prized possession for the sake of others. Each person then places the paper-promise in the manger or hangs it on the Christmas tree.

CHRISTMAS EVE SPRINKLE COOKIES

Cookies cut in holiday patterns — wreaths, stars, bells, and gingerbread men — and bedecked with plump raisins, creamy icing, and crunchy sugar crystals have been a part of Christmases around the world for generations.

It is also fitting and inspiring to make cookies in the shapes of a star, angels, a tree, a dove, and other related forms and then talk about the significance of each symbol to the Christmas story.

At our house, we prepare the sugar cookie dough ahead of time and have it ready and chilling in the refrigerator the afternoon of Christmas Eve. (See the back of the book for our recipes.) We keep on hand a box of assorted cookie cutters which is brought out of storage each Christmas. I also gather jars of red and green sprinkles, tiny silver balls, fresh juicy raisins, and several tubes of different flavors of icing.

We — and anyone else who stops by, including Grandma, favorite aunts and family friends — cut out and decorate tons of sprinkle cookies. Sometimes I wonder what we are going do to with all that huge pile of "tasty pastry," but somehow the cookies always seem to disappear. Some of them we eat as dessert with our simple Christmas Eve buffet, while others we deliver to families in the neighborhood, as well as to shut-ins and friends.

A BIRTHDAY CAKE FOR JESUS

A wonderful tradition is to make a small cake for Christmas Eve or Christmas Day. A tiny creche is placed on top of the cake, along with a single candle. Beside each plate is a special place card with a favorite Bible verse. Everyone then gathers around the table and sings "Happy Birthday to Jesus."

A CHRISTMAS WEB

This is a holiday scheme for gift distributing that originated in the Victorian era. In this game, parents prepare an untangling race which is enjoyed by children from preschoolers to teenagers. It is a lot of fun to play on Christmas Eve or Christmas Day, during a family holiday party, or at the home of a friend or relative.

First, you need a small gift or treat and a ball of string or yarn in a different color for each member of the family. Fasten a different color string to each of the gifts, hide them in various places, and then wind the string — looping around furniture, through chair legs and stair bannisters, over curtain rods, etc. — making a colorful and complicated web. (For older players you can make the web harder to untangle and the trail more difficult to follow.) All strings end at the doorway and are attached to strips of cardboard for rewinding.

Hand each player his cardboard spool and watch the fun as the strings are rewound and the gifts are discovered. The winner is the first person to find his gift, untangle the string, and wind it into a ball.

(If you have warm weather in December, you can even play this game outdoors.)

CHRISTMAS DAY GIFT-GIVING TRADITION

I heard the bells on Christmas day. . . .
Henry Wadsworth Longfellow

On Christmas morning you can separate all the gifts under the tree according to the *giver* rather the receiver. Then, one at a time, each giver gets to take a gift to its receiver. (Children love to deliver their presents to others.) This custom keeps the focus on giving instead of receiving.

CHRISTMAS MORNING BRUNCH

Each year, after opening our gifts on Christmas morning, my family and I have the same kind of tasty brunch: sticky-sweet cinnamon rolls, ice-cold orange juice and steaming hot coffee, along with an egg casserole I have whipped up the night before. (See recipe section for directions.)

You can make up your own brunch menu of your family favorites, which can be as elaborate and as varied from year to year as you like — from blueberry muffins and apple juice to crepes-suzette and cafe au lait. The most important thing is the tradition of having something special to eat and to share together as a family on that most special of all mornings of the year. The memories — the delicious smells, the mouth-watering tastes, and the happy moments spent together — will be recalled and savored over and over again through the years!

CHAPTER EIGHT

ADAPTING OLD TRADITIONS AND ADOPTING NEW ONES

There is a time for everything,
and a season for every activity
under heaven:

a time to be born and a time to die,
a time to plant and a time to uproot,. . .
a time to tear down and a time to build,
a time to weep and a time to laugh,
a time to mourn and a time to dance,
a time to scatter stones and a time
to gather them,
a time to embrace and a time to
refrain,
a time to search and a time to give
up,
a time to keep and a time to throw
away. . . .

Ecclesiastes 3:1-6 NIV

Family traditions at Christmas, or any other season, are lovely, but should not be set in concrete. Just as the family itself is dynamic — growing and changing with each new year — so traditions can be refreshed by a sense of flexibility and creativity as old ones are adapted or new ones are adopted to fit the changing needs and desires of the developing family.

Remember, the important thing is not having the "perfect" Christmas (which rarely, if ever happens), but rather in making the most of the time that we have with those we love, those who make Christmas — and indeed every day of our lives — so happy and blessed. These are the real gifts of Christmas.

"A TIME TO KEEP...A TIME TO THROW AWAY"

As my children grow up, I hope most of all to remember my favorite calligraphy message which says, "Lord, help me through the transitions that are yet to come!"

On the Friday night before Christmas, Holmes and I sat at the kitchen table working on our Christmas projects. It was just the two of us (and our Shelties asleep by the fire). Nearby the tree shone with colored lights and the New England Christmastide tape was playing, but otherwise the house was empty and quiet.

Our three teenagers were out, busy with their own activities: Justin was on a date; Chris was at a movie with friends; Alison was at her Bible study Christmas party for the evening. A few years earlier they would have been right at the table with us making ornaments. But in this season of our life, as inevitable changes come, it occurred to me that sometimes certain family traditions seem to be set aside for a few years as our children grow and become involved in other projects or activities.

We still enjoyed our tree-trimming night as a family, but even that was to be postponed two weeks until Justin got home from college, and then carefully worked into Alison's scheduled play rehearsal and performance at church. Not as many stories were read by the fire, for Chris and Alison (in high school and junior high) each had been assigned several hours of homework and research papers to do, besides Chris' school basketball games which lasted right up until the holiday. One of my favorite Christmastime activities is having people over, but this year we waited until *after* Christmas (and before New Year's) to invite our favorite guests for a time of holiday fellowship.

Some of our family traditions enjoyed when the children were younger have evolved into different customs. (Yet, encouragingly, some have remained the same year after year. We did make our sprinkle cookies on Christmas Eve, and gathered for the midnight service at church.) Our children no longer "dress up" as Mary and the shepherds to act out the Christmas pageant in the living room, as they once did, but we have started a new tradition of sharing around the table at Christmas dinner a special or humorous holiday memory and sponsoring a child in another country.

When seasons and traditions change, we may feel a sense of loss or a pang of nostalgia.

As my friend Dorothy says, "If there's no more joy in the tradition, if it's inconvenient because lifestyles change, we must be willing to open our hand and release it. Then when we do, new customs evolve."

But as our children grow up and begin their own families, perhaps some of the family traditions we enjoyed so much in the past will appear again — adapted or with a slightly different flavor — as part of their cherished Christmas celebrations.

OUT WITH THE OLD, IN WITH THE NEW!

"I will honour Christmas in my heart,
and try to keep it all the year. I will
live in the Past, the Present, and the Future."
Ebenezer Scrooge
Charles Dickens' "A Christmas Carol"

The Burshek family had always opened their presents on Christmas morning. But when their children grew up and married, they changed their gathering to Christmas Eve, starting a new tradition of enjoying a buffet dinner, attending the seven o'clock candlelight Communion service together at their church, and then coming home to open gifts with children, spouses, and grandchildren.

My friend Mary Mayer and her family had always had a few families over on Christmas Day for dinner. But when they moved to Chicago where they didn't know many people, they began a new tradition. After Christmas dinner they went to the center of the city and looked at the brightly decorated windows. Then they took a horse-drawn carriage ride through the downtown area, enjoying the Christmas lights and singing carols together.

When the Jordan family's children started going off to college, they began a new tradition of having their tree-trimming party at Thanksgiving when everyone was home.

A couple whose grown children are now scattered from Oregon to Florida invited a different young family each week to take part in their Advent wreath family worship time, make an ornament and share a holiday meal with them.

What is really important to you and your family? What shared activities or customs, if omitted, would keep Christmas from seeming like Christmas for you? Is it just spending time together, helping a needy family, extending hospitality to others? Is it making wreaths, doing craft work, decorating the house, attending the midnight service, or baking goodies on the days prior to Christmas? Sometimes we are made to realize what it is we love most about the holiday season when a busy schedule crowds out that particular activity.

It's a fine balance to be the "keeper of traditions" and yet still be open to change. If you and your family have begun to feel pressured or obligated to do things "just the way we have always done them," perhaps it is time to sit down and discuss the situation, asking family members what is most important to them, and seeing if anything needs to be changed.

If it makes everyone happy to get take-out or order-in Chinese food for Christmas Eve instead of having the traditional turkey dinner, then start a new family tradition. If it's traditional to troop downtown to shop for Grandpa's muffler together and the kids suddenly decide they hate to shop, then hire a sitter and go with your spouse and enjoy the outing with just the two of you.

The main thing is to be flexible and imaginative, to enjoy the gifts of the season. . . and to have a wonderful Christmas!

WHEN OUR PLANS GO ASTRAY

No matter how much time and effort we put into preparing to enjoy our favorite holiday activities and traditions with family and friends, often (as Robert Burns reminds us) the "best-laid plans" can and do go astray. Ours certainly have!

During special holiday times we can find ourselves in the midst of loss or grief, in the process of a cross-country move, or experiencing an unexpected illness or accident. But my family and I have found that even (*especially!*) these unforeseen circumstances can be opportunities for God's amazing love to spring forth in unlikely places and unexpected ways to touch our lives and draw us closer to Him and to each other!

"UNLIKELY PLACES"

In 1975 our four-year-old son Justin was in a hospital in Tulsa, Oklahoma, recovering from a severe asthma attack. We had planned to spend a very traditional family Christmas at home, but as it turned out our young son was one of the few patients in the children's ward who was just too ill to be released. Despite our carefully laid plans, it had become evident that Justin, along with a few other sick youngsters and their parents, would not be going home for the holidays.

The whole hospital experience had been painful for Justin. I felt sorry for him. Instead of sitting on Santa's knee sharing his Christmas wish, or hanging his stocking on the mantelpiece at home, there he was — stuck in a drab hospital, hooked up to an IV and caged by an oxygen tent.

Moreover, I was disappointed that my own last-minute plans for package-wrapping, cookie-baking, and stocking-stuffing had been spoiled. Being newcomers in town, we had no friends to visit us in the hospital, and despite the good intentions of the caring medical staff, a hospital was still a very lonely place to be at Christmas time.

I missed our other son, eighteen-month-old Christopher who was at home with Dad in our family room which, when we left, had been all aglow with twinkling Christmas tree lights, gaily colored felt stockings all hung in a row, bright plaid bows, and shining candles. In contrast, Justin and I gazed for hours at the monotonous brown walls and faded curtains that blended so well with the gray hospital floors.

I felt angry and frustrated, but I didn't want to show it. I needed to help keep Justin's spirits up until we could get him back home. The family had decided to postpone Christmas until the day Justin returned. Until then, we would act as if Christmas hadn't yet arrived.

While we had expected to put Christmas off, God had other plans! Much to our surprise, He was to use this experience to teach us the true meaning of Christmas.

On Christmas Eve, God's love came first in the form of a man brightly dressed as Santa Claus. Bounding down the hall, he delivered a thoughtful, personal gift to each youngster. Justin was given a cowboy hat that, surprisingly, was just his size.

"Who is this from?" I asked the nurse in attendance. "Did some organization send this gift?"

I thought that perhaps some local civic club had done this as its yearly project.

"On, no," she replied. "Three years ago a mom and dad's only daughter, a little three-year-old, died in this ward on Christmas Eve. Now each year the parents bring special gifts to the children who have to stay in the hospital at Christmas. Although they prefer to remain anonymous, they still manage to obtain the exact size or need of each child."

While I was pondering this act of kindness, two little Campfire girls brought in a handmade white mitten ornament decorated with holly and presented it to Justin.

"Merry Christmas!" they chimed to us as they continued happily down the hall.

Hardly had the cheerful words faded away when a family of Mexican-American carolers arrived. Gaily dressed in red and green native costumes, guitars in hand, they sang to us of the "Silent Night."

Next a big University of Oklahoma football player in his red and white varsity jersey walked in and began to chat with Justin. An avid football fan,

Justin couldn't believe that a "real live" gridiron hero had come especially to see him. He was all the more amazed and delighted when the burly athlete produced a surprise gift for him. Opening it, Justin beamed.

"A cowboy rifle and spurs!" he exclaimed excitedly. "They go with the hat!"

The coincidence took my breath away.

The next day, on Christmas morning, a tall, thin, shabbily dressed man quietly entered the room and sat on the edge of Justin's bed. Like some character from a Dickens novel, his clothes were tattered and torn. Without a word, he took out an old flute and began to play a lovely Christmas medley. One carol blended into another as the simplicity of each song took on a beauty beyond any I had ever known. Finishing his serenade like the little drummer boy, he handed Justin a small cup full of tiny red candles. Then with a smile, he slipped out the door. He had said very little and had never identified himself.

Slowly, but clearly, I began to realize that none of the people who had shared their love and gifts with us knew us — or had even told us their names. We had done nothing to earn or deserve their gifts. While my own hurts and needs had created a cold barrier around my emotions, these simple acts of kindness had caused the walls of neglected feelings to come tumbling down.

That lonely hospital, with its drab walls lined with construction paper bells, had become a place of God's healing and reconciling love. Away from family, friends, and our baby son, without our family tree and familiar traditions, God had delivered to us His special Christmas gift. The loneliest and darkest of places had been filled with the presence of angels and the brightest of lights.

RESOURCES, RECIPES AND RECOLLECTIONS

RESOURCES

CHRISTMAS STORIES AND BOOKS TO READ ALOUD OR TAPE

Alcott, Louisa May, "A Christmas Dream and How It Came True"

Allsburg, Chris, *The Polar Express*

Andersen, Hans Christian, "The Fir Tree"

Appel, David, and Hudson, Merle, *Raphael, The Herald Angel*

Bradford, Roark, "How Come Christmas"

Church, Francis P., "Yes, Virginia, There Is a Santa Claus"

Cleary, Beverly, "Ramona and the Three Wise Persons"

Dickens, Charles, *A Christmas Carol,* "Mr. Pickwick on the Ice" from *Pickwick Papers*

Hegg, Tom, *A Cup of Christmas Tea*

Henry, O., "The Gift of the Magi"

Keats, Ezra Jack, *The Little Drummer Boy*

Lagerlof, Selma, "The Legend of the Christmas Rose"

MacDonald, George, *The Gifts of the Christ Child*

Marshall, Peter, *Let's Keep Christmas*

Moore, Clement Clarke, "The Night Before Christmas"

Potter, Beatrix, "The Tailor of Gloucester"

Robinson, Barbara, *The Best Christmas Pageant Ever*

Russian tale, "Baboushka"

Thayer, Jane, "The Puppy Who Wanted a Boy"

Tolstoy, "Martin the Cobbler"

Another version of this tale was Corrie ten Boom's favorite Christmas story entitled "The Shoemaker's Christmas"

Van Dyke, Henry, *The Story of the Other Wise Man*

Wibberly, Leonard, *The Shepherd's Reward*

Wilder, Laura Ingalls, "Mr. Edwards Meets Santa Claus"

LEGENDS FROM AROUND THE WORLD

The Poinsettia
The Woodcutter and the Christ Child
The Bird Tree
Christmas Among the Animals (old Dutch tale)
The Legend of the Raven
The Rosemary Legend
The Christ Child and the Pine Tree
The Legend of Robin Red-Breast
The Legend of the Cat

Book and Calendar Resources

Posy Lough's 44-page booklet, *Christmas Decorations: Turning Family Treasures Into Traditions,* gives many ideas on how to transform everyday items of special significance — like your children's discarded toys, pine cones from a mountain trip or shells from a beach visit, and fabric from a favorite dress — into ornaments and decorations you'll treasure for years to come.

To order "MY VERY OWN NATIVITY SET" (patterns to cut out in felt or other material and instructions for creating your own eleven-piece nativity set), an ADVENT CALENDAR (cross-stitch or pen-and-ink drawings) and an ADVENT HEIRLOOM STOCKING (counted cross-stitch kit), write to: The Posy Collection, P.O. Box 394, Simsbury, Connecticut 06070.

Dobson, Shirley and Gaither, Gloria. *Let's Make a Memory.* Waco, Texas: Word Books, 1983.

Pelican Publishing Company (1101 Monroe Street, P.O. Box 189, Gretna, Louisiana 70053 (504)-368-1175) publishes a set of cute regional and ethnic Christmas books — such as *Cajun* (Hillbilly, Prairie, Texas, etc.) *Night Before Christmas* — which make wonderful folklore tales to be read to children or taped in appropriate dialect.

Another excellent source for Christmas stories, poems, and articles, primarily for adults and older children, is *The Guideposts Christmas Treasury*, a Bantam Book published by arrangement with Doubleday & Company, copyright 1972, 1982.

Resources for "Create Your Own Book"

Sundance Publishers
Newtown Road
P.O. Box 1326
Littleton, MA 01460

Bare Books
Treetop Publishing
P.O. Box 085567
Racine, WI 53408

Each book contains blank pages of white paper, a hard cover suitable for the child to design his own cover, and durable sewn pages.

Resources for Christmas Straw Manger Scene

Straw for the Manger

Make a crib or manger of brown paper. The empty manger is given a place of honor somewhere at home. A piece of straw is placed in the manger for every kind act performed during Advent. The Baby Jesus (a tiny plastic baby doll wrapped in cloth) is not placed in the crib until Christmas Eve. By that time the crib is filled with soft straw.

Making the Manger

1. Cut out manger.
2. Fold paper in half lengthwise. Open.
3. Fold in each end along line A. Open.
4. Cut off corner triangles. Save them.
5. Cut in approximately 2'' from each end on center fold.
6. Fold cardboard in half lengthwise and cut 5/8'' from center on each end fold. Open.
7. Fold cardboard so that end triangles overlap.
8. Glue cut off triangles together in pairs.
9. Slip cut off triangles into slots at each end of manger. Glue in place.

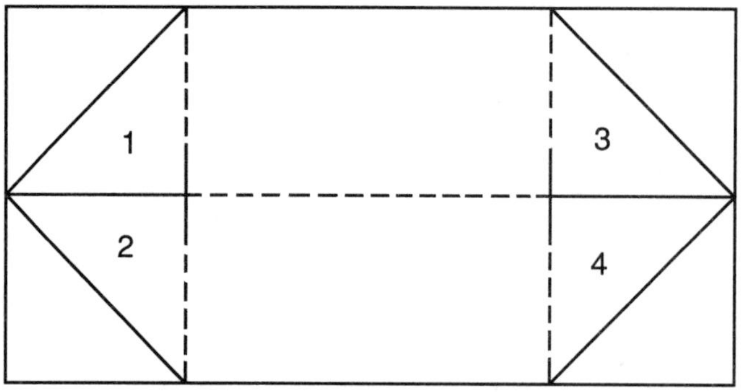

Glue on solid lines. Fold on broken lines.

SERVICE ORGANIZATIONS

Reputable agencies with worthwhile programs for sponsoring and/or assisting needy children around the world are:

CHRISTIAN CHILDREN'S FUND
P.O. Box 26511
Richmond, VA 23261

COMPASSION INTERNATIONAL
P.O. Box 7000
Colorado Springs, CO 80933

FEED THE CHILDREN
P.O. Box 36
Oklahoma City, OK 73101-0036
(405) 942-0228

SAVE THE CHILDREN
54 Wilton Road
Westport, CN 06880

UNICEF (which also sells wonderful Christmas cards)
3 United Nations Plaza
New York, NY 10017

WORLD VISION CHILDCARE
Pasadena, CA 91131

RECIPES

FAVORITE RECIPES FOR CHRISTMAS DISHES

Christmas Eve is a good time to celebrate your family's heritage with a special dish. Caroline Oda prepares *miso* soup with rice, smoked salmon and pickled herring to celebrate the Japanese side of her family heritage. Another friend serves rice pudding from an old family recipe (with an almond hidden inside, a Norwegian custom). Spiced or glazed pecans, a favorite dessert from Grandmother's recipe book (see below), can become a traditional Christmas Eve or Christmas Day fare. At the end of the recipe section is a place to record *your* family's traditional or ethnic recipes.

CHRISTMAS COOKIE RECIPES

These recipes were shared with me some years ago by the best cook I know, Cynthia Morris, and have been used by our family year after year:

Cut-Out Sugar Cookies

1 cup butter
1 cup sugar
1 egg
2 teaspoons vanilla
2 cups flour
1/2 teaspoon baking soda
1/2 teaspoon cream of tartar

Cream butter and sugar. Add egg and vanilla. Sift dry ingredients and mix to form dough. Refrigerate 2 balls of dough covered until ready to roll out and cut into Christmas cookies. Bake at 350 degrees until lightly browned, cool and decorate.

Roll-Out Sprinkle Cookies

1 cup butter
1 cup sugar
2 egg yolks
1 teaspoon vanilla
1/2 teaspoon salt
3 cups flour
1 teaspoon baking powder
1/3 cup milk

Cream butter and sugar. Add vanilla and egg yolks. Add dry ingredients and milk. Refrigerate three patties of dough until ready to roll out (wrapped or covered with waxed paper). Roll out approximately 1/4'' thick on a lightly floured board. Cut out shapes with floured cookie cutters.

Before baking, decorate cookies with green or red sprinkles, silver balls, or cinnamon candies. Bake at 350 to 375 degrees for 10 minutes or until lightly golden. After baking, decorate with icing from a tube or pastry bag.

Star of Bethlehem

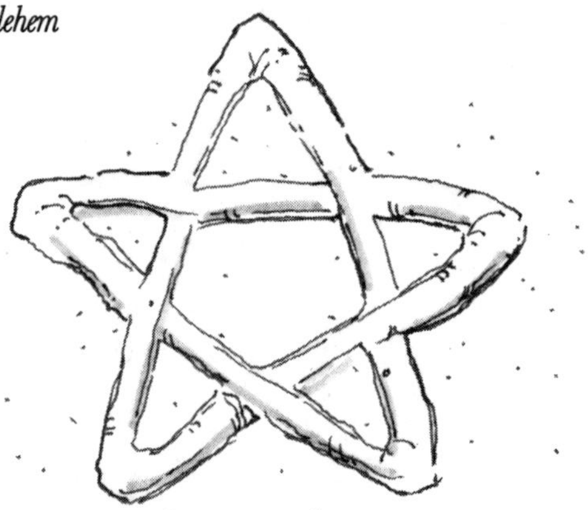

Here's something fun to make with leftover pie dough. You will need a cup of dough. Roll out the pastry and cut into five strips the same size. Arrange the strips in a star shape on a greased piece of aluminum foil on a cookie sheet. Pat together where the strips overlap to seal dough.

Crush some candies (clear-colored, hard candy works best) in a zip-lock bag or clean kitchen towel. Use the crushed candy chips to fill the open areas between the pastry. Separate the colors so they won't melt together. Bake the Star of Bethlehem in a 400-degree oven for about 12 minutes or until the candy is melted. After the star is cool, peel away the foil.

Christmas Stained-Glass Cookies

Colorful Christmas cookies which can be used for eating or for ornaments to string on a cookie tree or across a window are *Christmas Stained-Glass Cookies.*

Ingredients:

Cookie dough: "Cut-Out Sugar Cookie" recipe above
1/3 cup or more crushed colored hard candies

Separate colors of hard candy and put each color in a freezer bag and crush.

Preheat oven to 375 degrees. Make dough according to "Cut-Out Sugar Cookies" recipe. After chilling for 2 to 3 hours, roll out dough to 1/8" thickness on lightly floured board. Cut out cookies using large Christmas cookie cutters.

Transfer cookies to a foil-lined baking sheet. Using a small Christmas cookie cutter of the same shape as the large one, cut out and remove dough from the center of each cookie. Fill cut-out sections with crushed candy. If using cookies as hanging ornaments, you can make holes at top of cookies for string.

Bake 7 to 9 minutes or until cookies are lightly browned and candy melted. Slide foil off baking sheets, and when cool, carefully loosen cookies from foil.

CHRISTMAS MORNING CASSEROLE

This recipe is great because it can be made up ahead of time and cooked while the packages are being unwrapped:

1 lb. mild sausage
6 eggs
2 cups milk
1 teaspoon salt
1 teaspoon dry mustard
2 slices cubed white bread
1 cup shredded cheese

Brown sausage and drain well. Beat eggs. Add milk, salt, mustard. Gently stir in cheese, sausage, and bread. Place in buttered 9" x 13" casserole. Refrigerate overnight (at least 6 hours). Place in cold oven set at 350 degrees. Bake 45 minutes. Serve and enjoy for Christmas brunch.

OLD-FASHIONED GINGERBREAD

1/2 cup margarine
1/2 cup sugar
1 egg
2 1/2 cups sifted all-purpose flour
1 1/2 teaspoons baking soda
1 teaspoon ginger
1/2 teaspoon ground cloves
1/2 teaspoon salt
1 cup molasses
1 cup hot water
1 teaspoon cinnamon

Cream together margarine and sugar. Add egg and beat well. Sift together flour, baking soda, cinnamon, ginger, cloves, and salt. Combine molasses and water; add alternately with flour mixture to creamed mixture. Pour batter into well-greased and -floured 8" x 8" pan. Bake at 350 degrees for 50-60 minutes.

May be served warm with whipped cream or ice cream.

(EASY) HOLIDAY CRANBERRY FROZEN SALAD

Mix 1 can whole cranberry sauce and a 9-oz. can of drained, crushed pineapple with 8 ounces of sour cream blended with 1/4 cup confectioner's sugar. Mix well, pour in 9" x 12" pan and freeze.

Great to make ahead and serve — cut in squares — with any holiday meal.

CRANBERRY BREAD

2 cups flour, sifted
1 1/2 teaspoon baking powder
1/2 teaspoon soda
1 cup sugar
2 tablespoons salad oil
1 egg
1 cup raw, diced cranberries
1 cup pecans, chopped
1 orange
boiling water

Sift into mixing bowl: flour, baking powder, soda and sugar. Put into measuring cup, juice and grated rind of 1 orange; add in the cup 2 tablespoons salad oil and fill cup with boiling water.

Pour into dry ingredients and mix well. Add 1 whole egg and beat 1 minute. Stir by hand 1 cup diced cranberries and 1 cup pecans. Preheat oven to 325 degrees. Grease and flour pan. Pour in mixture. Bake about 1 1/4 hour. Test with straw in center. Store 24 hours before cutting. Makes 1 loaf.

CHRISTMAS MORNING COFFEE CAKE

2 1/4 cups all-purpose flour
1/2 teaspoon baking powder
1/2 teaspoon soda
1/2 teaspoon salt
1 cup buttermilk
1/2 cup butter
1 1/2 cups sugar
2 eggs
1 teaspoon vanilla

Sift dry ingredients. Cream butter and sugar. Add eggs, one at a time, and vanilla. Add buttermilk alternately with dry ingredients to creamed mixture.

Streusel Topping

1 cup brown sugar
1 tablespoon cinnamon
1 cup chopped nuts
4 tablespoons butter
4 tablespoons flour

Grease and flour 8" x 12" or 9" x 13" pan. Spread half of batter. Sprinkle half of streusel. Repeat. Bake at 350 degrees for 30-40 minutes.

COMPANY MASHED POTATOES

8 medium potatoes
(mashed with milk and butter)
8 oz. cream cheese
1 medium jar pimento
1 cup chopped onion
1 teaspoon salt
1 raw egg, beaten
dash pepper

Mix and bake at 350 degrees for 45 minutes.

Great to make ahead for Christmas dinner or potluck supper.

STRAWBERRY BREAD

3 cups flour
2 cups sugar
1 teaspoon baking soda
1 teaspoon salt
1 cup chopped pecans (optional)
2 10-oz. packages frozen strawberries, defrosted
4 eggs
1 cup oil

Mix all ingredients. Bake at 350 degrees for 50 minutes to 1 hour. Makes 2 loaves.

For a delicious icing, use 8 ounces cream cheese and juice from the strawberries.

Wrap loaves in red cellophane and tie with a ribbon for a lovely gift.

CRANBERRY ORANGE RELISH

Put through food chopper, blender or food processor:

4 cups cranberries
1 large orange (pulp and rind)
1 apple (optional)
1/2 cup chopped nuts (optional)

Mix together with 2 cups sugar and let stand several hours.

Great for serving with Christmas dinner or giving in a pretty jar as a gift.

FRUIT CAKE

1 lb. dates
1/2 lb. coconut
4 oz. red candied cherries
4 oz. green candied cherries
2 cups pecans
1 handful flour
1 can Eagle Brand milk

Chop dates and cherries coarsely. Mix with flour to coat fruit. Add nuts, milk, and coconut. Mix. Grease pan. Pour in mixture. Bake at 300 degrees for 45 minutes to 1 hour until brown. Freezes well.

CHEX MIX

6 tablespoons butter
4 teaspoons worcestershire sauce
3/8 teaspoon garlic powder
3/8 teaspoon salt
6 cups cereal (Corn, Rice, Wheat Chex, & Cheerios)
3/4 cup salted mixed nuts
1 1/2 cups pretzels

Heat oven to 250 degrees. Melt butter in a shallow pan. Stir in worcestershire sauce, garlic and salt. Mix in cereal and heat 45 minutes in oven, stirring every 15 minutes. While hot, add nuts and pretzels.

Alternative: Microwave on high for 6 minutes, stirring every 2 minutes.

Chex Mix is easy to whip up, makes a good snack for a party or gathering, and serves as a good gift — in a bright holiday tin.

CHOCOLATE TURTLES

1 14-oz. bag Kraft caramels
2 tablespoons water
2 tablespoons butter
2 cups chopped pecans
2 oz. paraffin
1 12-oz. package chocolate chips

Melt caramels in top of double boiler with water. Stir in pecans. Drop by teaspoons on buttered waxed paper. Refrigerate until firm enough to remove from paper. Melt chocolate and paraffin in top of double boiler. Dip caramels in chocolate mixture with fork. Place on waxed paper and do not refrigerate.

Wonderful gift!

CAROLER'S PUNCH (HOT WASSAIL)

Here's a recipe for caroler's punch that warms our fingers and throats after a delightful evening spent singing in the frosty air:

1 cup sugar
3 cups water
4 cinnamon sticks
1 tablespoon of cloves and allspice
12 ounces frozen orange juice and lemonade dissolved in 6 cups of water

Mix the above ingredients and bring to a boil, simmer one hour, remove the spices, serve and enjoy!

SWEET POTATO CASSEROLE

3 cups cooked sweet potatoes
1 cup sugar
1/2 cup milk
1/2 stick butter (melted)
1 teaspoon vanilla
1 teaspoon salt
2 eggs

Mix above ingredients and pour into casserole dish. Sprinkle with topping.

Topping

1 cup brown sugar
1 cup chopped pecans
1/3 cup flour
1/2 stick margarine

Mix dry ingredients and sprinkle on top of potatoes. Slice margarine into small pieces and lay on topping. Bake at 325 degrees for 25-30 minutes.

PEANUT BUTTER COOKIES

1 package prepared peanut butter cookie dough

1 package miniature peanut butter cups

Cut cookie dough into 9 slices. Divide each slice into quarters. Place each quarter into miniature muffin tin. Bake 8 to 10 minutes at 350 degrees. Remove from oven. While still hot, insert 1 miniature peanut butter cup into each cookie. Return to oven for 1 minute or until peanut butter cup is softened, Remove, cool and serve.

SPICED PECANS

Cook together:

1 cup sugar

1/2 cup water

1 teaspoon cinnamon

1/4 teaspoon salt

Use medium heat and stir. Boil until mixture reaches 230 degrees on candy thermometer. Remove from heat and stir in:

1 teaspoon vanilla

2 1/2 cups pecan halves

Mix well. Empty onto buttered cookie sheet, separate pecans and cool.

FRESH COCONUT CAKE

1 box Duncan Hines butter cake mix

4 whole eggs

1 can coconut

1 carton sour cream

2/3 cup sugar

3/4 cup buttery Wesson oil

1 teaspoon vanilla

Mix all ingredients except eggs. Add 1 egg at a time, beating after each one. Grease two 9'' cake pans and pour in mixture. Bake at 350 degrees for 15-20 minutes or until done.

Icing

1 1/2 cups sugar
1/8 teaspoon cream of tartar
2/3 cup water

Mix and cook until a thread can be spun with the mixture. Beat 3 egg whites until stiff. Pour sugar syrup over beaten egg whites, continually beating until glossy. Spread over cake, using coconut between layers and on top and sides.

ALMOND BARK CRUNCH (very easy)

1 pound almond bark white chocolate
2 tablespoons shortening
3 cups pretzel sticks
1 cup salted Spanish peanuts

Mix together chocolate and shortening in the top of a double boiler; bring water to a boil. Reduce heat to low; cook mixture until chocolate melts. Pour mixture into a large bowl. Stir in pretzels and peanuts; spread onto a buttered cookie sheet. Chill until firm. Break into pieces. Store in an airtight container. Recipe yields 1 1/2 pounds.

CHRISTMAS FUDGE

Fudge is a festive gift or dessert for the holidays:

2 1/2 cups sugar
3/4 cup Pet milk
16 large marshmallows
or 1 cup marshmallow cream
1/2 teaspoon salt
6 oz. (1 cup) semi-sweet chocolate pieces
1 cup pecans, chopped
1 teaspoon vanilla
1/2 cup butter or margarine

Mix in a heavy 2-quart saucepan sugar, milk, marshmallows or marshmallow cream, butter or margarine and salt. Cook, stirring constantly over medium heat until mixture comes to a boil (starts bubbling all over the top). Boil and stir 5 minutes more. Remove from heat. Add the semi-sweet chocolate pieces and stir until completely melted. Stir in pecans and vanilla. Spread on a buttered 8-inch-square pan. Cool and cut into 30 pieces.

CARROT CAKE

2 cups sugar
1 1/4 cups Wesson oil
3 cups grated carrots
4 eggs
dash of salt
1 teaspoon vanilla
2 cups flour
2 teaspoons cinnamon
2 teaspoons baking soda
1/2 teaspoon baking powder
1 cup crushed pineapple (not drained)

Mix all ingredients together and bake at 350 degrees for 45 minutes to 1 hour.

Icing

1 stick oleo
1 8-oz. package cream cheese
1 box powdered sugar
1 teaspoon vanilla
3/4 cup finely chopped pecans
3/4 cup coconut

Put first 4 ingredients in mixer and beat until creamy. Add pecans and coconut.

CHRISTMAS CHEESE CAKE

4 8-oz. packages cream cheese
1 1/4 cups sugar
5 eggs
1 teaspoon vanilla

Cream cheese until it becomes smooth, then add eggs 1 at a time with a little sugar. Add vanilla. Beat at high speed for 5 minutes. Pour into 10'' cheese cake pan and bake at 325 degrees for 45 minutes to 1 hour. When the sides begin to brown, check to see if the middle is firm. If so, pour on topping, turn off oven and leave for 15 minutes. Remove from oven and let cool.

Topping

1 pint sour cream
1/4 cup sugar
1 teaspoon vanilla

Blend ingredients together and pour on cake when done.

Crust

1 1/4 cups graham cracker crumbs
1/4 cup butter or margarine
(melted)
1/4 cup sugar

Press firmly together in pan.

Top individual servings with fruit or pour on flavored syrups. (Blackberry syrup is a wonderful addition!)

NEW ZEALAND PAVLOVA

3 egg whites
1 teaspoon cold water
1 cup sugar
1 teaspoon vanilla
1 teaspoon vinegar
1 carton whipping cream

Beat egg whites and water together until very thick. Gradually add sugar, beating constantly. Fold in vanilla and vinegar.

Spoon onto dry brown paper or oven tray. Heat oven to 450 degrees. Put Pavlova into oven and turn off. Leave in oven overnight (or until oven is cool).

Remove and cover with whipped cream.

CHERRY CHOCOLATE CAKE

1 teaspoon almond flavoring
1 box chocolate cake mix
1 can cherry pie filling
3 eggs

Mix all ingredients together. Pour mixture into a 9" x 13" (or sheet) cake pan. Bake at 350 degrees for 35 to 40 minutes. Allow to cool.

Frosting

1 cup sugar
5 tablespoons margarine
1/3 cup milk

Mix ingredients and boil for 1 minute. Add 6 ounces of chocolate chips. Pour mixture on cake.

FRIENDSHIP LEMON CAKE

3/4 cup (1 1/2 sticks) butter (or corn oil margarine)
2 cups superfine granulated sugar (1 lb. box)
4 eggs
2 lemons (grated rind for cake, juice for topping)
1 cup milk (lowfat is fine)
3 cups presifted flour
2 teaspoons baking powder
1/2 teaspoon salt
2 cups chopped nuts

Cream butter with sugar. Add eggs 1 at a time, beating well after each addition. Add grated lemon rind. Mix flour, salt and baking powder. *Then* add alternately with the milk to the creamed butter, beginning with the flour.

Spoon onto lightly greased and floured pans. Bake at 350 degrees for 40-60 minutes. Makes 3 loaves.

Topping

2/3 cup sugar
juice of 2 lemons

Drizzle topping over cakes when they come out of the oven.

To serve, warm slightly and butter.

KACHINA COOKIES

1/3 cup safflower oil & 1 stick margarine
1 1/2 cup raw honey
2 eggs
4 tablespoons instant dry milk
1 cup peanut butter
4 teaspoons vanilla
2 teaspoons soda
1/2 teaspoons salt
2 1/2 cup whole wheat pastry flour

Mix oil, margarine (softened), and honey. Beat in 2 eggs and dry milk. Blend in peanut butter and vanilla, mixing well. Then separately mix dry ingredients (soda, salt, and whole wheat flour), and add the wet mixture. Drop by large teaspoonfuls onto a cookie sheet, and bake at 300 degrees for 10 minutes.

Makes a very nutritious and festive cookie!

CINNAMON APPLE MUFFINS

2 1/2 cups flour
3 1/2 teaspoons baking powder
1/2 teaspoon cinnamon
4 tablespoons shortening
1/2 cup sugar
2 eggs, beaten
1 cup milk
3 cups finely chopped apples
1 teaspoon salt

Cream shortening and sugar. Add eggs. Add dry ingredients and milk, alternately. Mix 2 tablespoons sugar and 1 teaspoon cinnamon. Sprinkle on top. Bake at 450 degrees for 20-25 minutes. Makes 72 mini-muffins.

Great for mother-daughter tea or neighborhood Christmas coffee.

CHOCOLATE OATMEAL PEANUT BUTTER COOKIES

2 cups sugar
2-3 tablespoons cocoa
1/4 pound oleo
1/2 cup milk
1 cup chunky peanut butter
2 cups oatmeal
1 teaspoon vanilla

Mix sugar, cocoa, oleo and milk together in a large saucepan. Bring to a boil over medium heat. Boil for *1 minute.* Immediately add peanut butter, oatmeal and vanilla.

Beat by hand until dough starts to stiffen. Drop by spoonfuls onto an ungreased cookie sheet.

Serve after cookies cool and harden.

A GINGERBREAD FANTASY: HOW TO MAKE A GINGERBREAD HOUSE

This gingerbread house is totally edible. It makes a wonderful gift for the family with children. Kids love to decorate it, and to eat the candy and gingerbread as they work, so make extra cookies for munching.

First, make a pattern on graph paper. Then cut the pieces out of waxed paper to use on the dough: two each of the sides, one back, one front and two roof pieces. Take heavy cardboard and cover with foil the size you want the yard of the house to be.

To Make Gingerbread Dough

5 1/2 cups sifted all-purpose flour
1 teaspoon baking soda
1 teaspoon salt
1 tablespoon cinnamon
2 teaspoons ginger
2 teaspoons cloves
1 teaspoon nutmeg
1 cup shortening
1 cup sugar
1 cup molasses
1 egg

1. Sift flour, baking soda, salt, cinnamon, ginger, cloves, and nutmeg onto waxed paper.

2. Beat shortening with sugar until light and fluffy. Beat in molasses and egg. Stir in flour mixture to make a stiff dough. Chill several hours or overnight until firm enough to roll.

3. Roll out the dough and lay the patterns on it. Cut out the shapes.* Bake at 350 degrees until golden brown and very spongy when lightly touched with finger. Cool completely.

*If you have leftover dough, you can make cookies. Roll 1/8'' thick, cut out, and bake 15 to 20 minutes. Decorate with any leftover frosting, raisins, redhots, or candy.

To Make Royal Frosting

4 egg whites
5 1/2 cups confectioner's sugar
1 teaspoon cream of tartar
1 teaspoon clear vanilla (optional for taste)

Beat eggs until they rise and become fluffy. Gradually add sugar and cream of tartar (and clear vanilla). Mix well.

To Make Sugar Cement

Put 3-4 cups of white sugar in a skillet and melt it on high, stirring constantly. It will turn brown. You will keep the sugar cement hot on the stove while dipping the edges, sides, and roof of the house in the cement before assembling the pieces. You will also glue the house to the cardboard with the sugar cement. Sugar cement is used instead of glue so the house will be safe to eat.

To Assemble Gingerbread House

Dip the edge of the cookie pieces (roof, sides, etc.) into hot sugar cement, and then quickly press together.

Decorate the house any way you desire using any royal frosting. (Any cracks or breaks can be covered with frosting, and no one will notice.) Use cookies on the roof, or press rock candy in the windows while the dough is still hot. Marshmallows can be used in many ways. At Christmas time there are lots of different holiday candies available for use in decorating: Make a ribbon candy fence (out of candy cane sticks); use gumdrops, M&Ms, licorice or peppermint pieces for the roof.

Christmas is a wonderful time to celebrate your family heritage with a special food or activity. Record your family traditions or recipes brought from another country, or record one you would like to begin from your family's ethnic or regional origin.

GINGERBREAD HOUSE

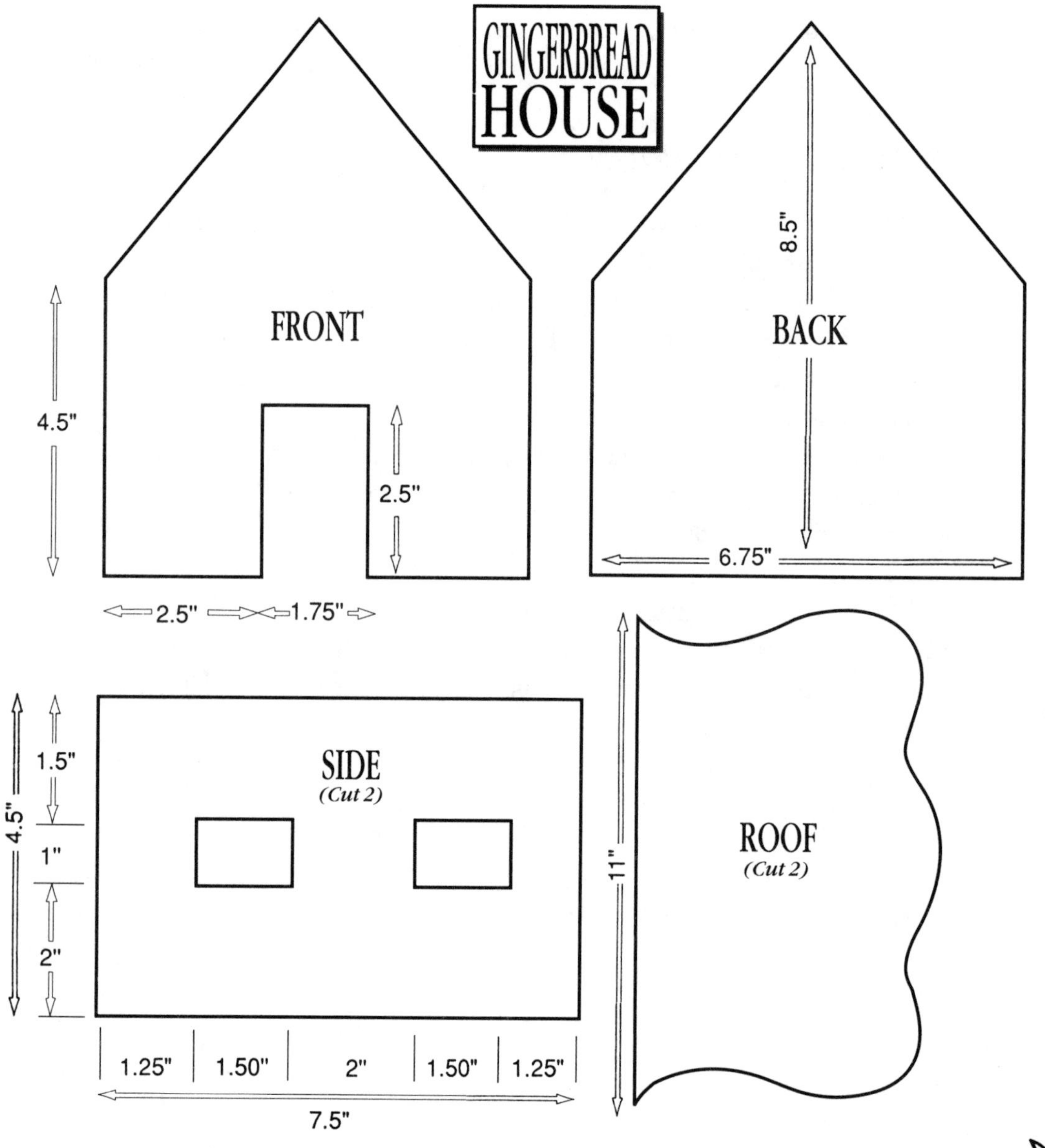

RECOLLECTIONS

FAMILY DISCUSSION

Have a family discussion about Christmas and your own traditions. These questions might start the discussion:

1. What have you enjoyed *most* (and *least*) that we have done in the past?

2. What holiday activities, if discontinued, would make it not seem like Christmas to you?

3. What is one thing you would like to change in next year's celebration?

4. What kind of service (community, church, neighborhood, family, charity) would you like to do next year?

5. Who would you like for us to invite over to share in our holiday festivities?

6. Which of our holiday traditions would you like to carry on in your family when you grow up?

7. What kind of gift can you give someone that is not bought in a store? How can we give ourselves this Christmas?

You might also discuss the following:

Name a new tradition that you would like to try from each of these sections:

Advent:

Service:

Hospitality:

Tree-trimming:

Ornament-making:

Gift-giving:

ONCE UPON A TIME — CHRISTMAS STORYTELLING

A well-told story is a love-gift from parent or grandparent to a child. Spend some time reflecting on your past experiences and family stories that were passed down to you. Then find a cozy place next to the fireplace and relate a story to your children. You might consider: How did you celebrate birthdays, Christmas, and Thanksgiving when you were young? Which Christmas stands out in your memory, and why? What was the best gift you ever received?

CREATING YOUR OWN FAMILY CHRISTMAS JOURNAL

Keep a five-year journal of Christmas activities and memories. Suggestions for topics to include are listed below.

A cloth-covered blank book makes a good place for your Christmas journal. Entries can include (each taking a separate page or pages):

- Christmas Memories

  Christmas is a time for remembering . . .

  Write down your favorite Christmas memories, those you would like to preserve and pass on to your children and grandchildren. (Let each person in the family write down his own special Christmas memories. They can be humorous, surprising, poignant. . . . Little one's favorite memories can be dictated to Mom or Dad and recorded.)

- Ethnic Traditions/Family Heritage
- Christmas Projects/Activities
- Holiday Trips and Visits
- Special Guests
- Memorable Holiday Happenings
- How We Spent Christmas Eve
- How We Spent Christmas Day
- Paste in your family photo for each year

CHRISTMAS JOURNAL

Ethnic Traditions/Family Heritage:

Christmas Projects/Activities:

Holiday Trips and Visits:

Special Guests:

Memorable Holiday Happenings:

How We Spent Christmas Eve:

How We Spent Christmas Day:

Paste in your family photo for each year

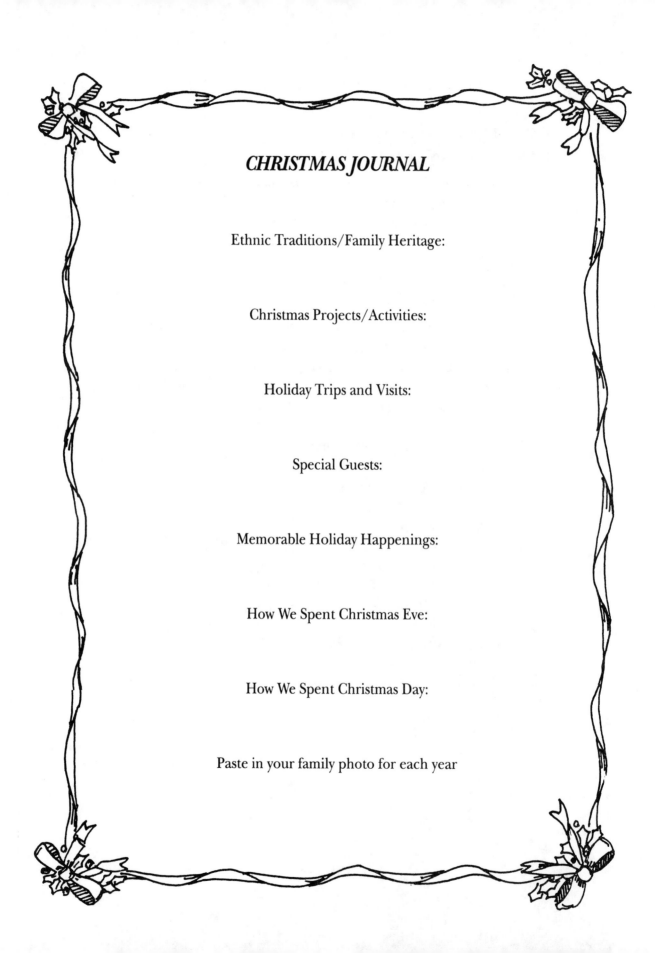

THE CHRISTMAS STORY

About this time Caesar Augustus, the Roman Emperor, decreed that a census should be taken throughout the nation. (This census was taken when Quirinius was governor of Syria.)

Everyone was required to return to his ancestral home for this registration. And because Joseph was a member of the royal line, he had to go to Bethlehem in Judea, King David's ancient home — journeying there from the Galilean village of Nazareth. He took with him Mary, his fiancee, who was obviously pregnant by this time.

And while they were there, the time came for her baby to be born; and she gave birth to her first child, a son. She wrapped him in a blanket and laid him in a manger, because there was no room for them in the village inn.

That night some shepherds were in the fields outside the village, guarding their flocks of sheep. Suddenly an angel appeared among them, and the landscape shone bright with the glory of the Lord. They were badly frightened, but the angel reassured them.

"Don't be afraid!" he said. "I bring you the most joyful news ever announced, and it is for everyone! The Savior — yes, the Messiah, the Lord — has been born tonight in Bethlehem! How will you recognize him? You will find a baby wrapped in a blanket, lying in a manger!"

Suddenly, the angel was joined by a vast host of others — the armies of heaven — praising God:

"Glory to God in the highest heaven," they sang, "and peace on earth for all those pleasing him."

When this great army of angels had returned again to heaven, the shepherds said to each other, "Come on! Let's go to Bethlehem! Let's see this wonderful thing that has happened, which the Lord has told us about."

They ran to the village and found their way to Mary and Joseph. And there was the baby, lying in the manger. The shepherds told everyone what had happened and what the angel had said to them about this child. All who heard the shepherds' story expressed astonishment, but Mary quietly treasured these things in her heart and often thought about them.

Then the shepherds went back again to their fields and flocks, praising God for the visit of the angels, and because they had seen the child, just as the angel had told them.

Luke 2:1-20 TLB

FAVORITE CHRISTMAS SONGS

O LITTLE TOWN OF BETHLEHEM

Phillips Brooks (1835-1893) Lewis H. Redner (1831-1908)

O little town of Bethlehem,
How still we see thee lie!
Above thy deep and dreamless sleep
The silent stars go by;
Yet in thy dark streets shineth
The everlasting Light;
The hopes and fears of all the years
Are met in thee tonight.

For Christ is born of Mary,
And gathered all above,
While mortals sleep the angels keep
Their watch of wond'ring love.
O morning stars together
Proclaim the holy birth,
And praises sing to God the King,
And peace to men on earth!

How silently, how silently,
The wond'rous gift is giv'n!
So God imparts to human hearts
The blessing of His heav'n.
No ear may hear His coming,
But in this world of sin,
Where meek souls will receive Him still,
The Dear Christ enters in.

O holy Child of Bethlehem,
Descend to us, we pray;
Cast out our sin and enter in;
Be born in us today!
We hear the Christmas angels
The great glad tidings tell;
O come to us, abide with us
Our Lord Emmanuel!

WE THREE KINGS OF ORIENT ARE

John Henry Hopkins Jr. (1820-1891)

We three kings of Orient are,
Bearing gifts we traverse afar,
Field and fountain, moor and mountain,
Following yonder star.

Refrain: O Star of wonder, star of night,
Star with royal beauty bright,
Westward leading, still proceeding,
Guide us to thy perfect light.

Born a King on Bethlehem's plain,
Gold I bring to crown Him again,
King forever, ceasing never
Over us all to reign.

Refrain.

Frankincense to offer have I,
Incense owns a Deity nigh:
Prayer and praising all men raising,
Worship Him, God on high.

Refrain.

Myrrh is mine; its bitter perfume
Breathes a life of gathering gloom;
Sorrowing, sighing, bleeding, dying,
Sealed in the stone-cold tomb.

Refrain.

Glorious now behold Him arise,
King, and God, and sacrifice;
Heaven sings alleluia:
Alleluia the earth replies.

Refrain.

WHAT CHILD IS THIS?

William Chatterton Dix (1837-1898) 16th-century English

What child is this, Who laid to rest,
On Mary's lap is sleeping?
Whom angels greet with anthems sweet,
While shepherds' watch are keeping?

Refrain: This, this is Christ the King,
Whom shepherds guard and angels sing:
This, this is Christ the King,
The Babe, the Son of Mary.

Why lies He in such mean estate,
Where ox and ass are feeding?
Good Christian, fear: for sinners here
The silent Word is pleading.

Refrain.

So bring Him incense, gold, and myrrh,
Come, peasant, king to own Him;
The King of kings, salvation brings,
Let loving hearts enthrone him.

Refrain.

IT CAME UPON A MIDNIGHT CLEAR

Edmund H. Sears (1810-1876) Richard S. Willis (1819-1900)

It came upon a midnight clear,
That glorious song of old,
From angels bending near the earth
To touch their harps of gold;
"Peace on the earth, good will to men,
From heav'n's all gracious King."
The world in solemn stillness lay
To hear the angels sing.

Still through the cloven skies they come,
With peaceful wings unfurled,
And still their heav'nly music floats
O'er all the weary world;
Above its sad and lowly plains
They bend on hov'ring wing,
And ever o'er its Babel sounds
The blessed angels sing.

O ye beneath life's crushing load,
Whose forms are bending low,
Who toil along the climbing way,
With painful steps and slow,
Look now, for glad and golden hours
Come swiftly on the wing:
O rest beside the weary road,
And hear the angels sing!

For lo! the days are hast'ning on,
By prophets seen of old,
When with the ever circling years,
Shall come the time foretold,
When the new heav'n and earth shall own
The Prince of Peace their King,
And the whole world send back the song
Which now the angels sing.

SILENT NIGHT

Joseph Mohr (1792-1848) Franz Xavier Gruber (1787-1863)

Silent night, holy night!
All is calm, all is bright
Round yon Virgin Mother and Child.
Holy Infant so tender and mild,
Sleep in heavenly peace,
Sleep in heavenly peace.

HARK! THE HEARLD ANGELS SING

Charles Wesley (1707-1788) Felix Mendelssohn-Bartholdy (1809-1847)

Hark! the herald angels sing,
"Glory to the new-born King;
Peace on earth, and mercy mild,
God and sinners reconciled!"
Joyful, all ye nations, rise,
Join the triumph of the skies;
With angelic hosts proclaim,
"Christ is born in Bethlehem!"

Refrain: Hark! the herald angels sing,
"Glory to the new-born King."

Christ, by highest heaven adored;
Christ, the everlasting Lord;
Come, Desire of Nations, come,
Fix in us thy humble home.
Veiled in flesh the God-head see;
Hail th'Incarnate Deity,
Pleased as man with man to dwell;
Jesus, our Emmanuel.

Refrain.

Hail, the heav'n-born Prince of Peace!
Hail, the Sun of Righteousness!
Light and life to all He brings,
Ris'n with healing in His wings;
Mild He lays His glory by,
Born that man no more may die,
Born to raise the sons of earth,
Born to give them second birth.

Refrain.

ANGELS WE HAVE HEARD ON HIGH

Traditional French

Angels we have heard on high,
Sweetly singing o'er the plains,
And the mountains in reply,
Echoing their joyful strains,
Gloria in excelsis Deo,
Gloria in excelsis Deo.

Shepherds why this jubilee?
Why your joyous strains prolong?
What the gladsome tidings be?
Which inspire your heav'nly song?
Gloria in excelsis Deo,
Gloria in excelsis Deo.

Come to Bethlehem and see
Him whose birth the angels sing;
Come, adore on bended knee,
Christ the Lord, the newborn King.
Gloria in excelsis Deo,
Gloria in excelsis Deo.

THE FIRST NOEL

Traditional

The first Noel, the angel did say,
Was to certain poor shepherds in fields
as they lay;
In fields where they lay keeping their sheep,
On a cold winter's night that was so deep.

Refrain: Noel, Noel, Noel, Noel,
Born is the King of Israel.

They looked up and saw a star
Shining in the east, beyond them far,
And to the earth it gave great light,
And so it continued both day and night.

Refrain.

And by the light of that same star
Three wisemen came from country far;
To seek for a King was their intent,
And to follow the star wherever it went.

Refrain.

This star drew nigh to the northwest,
O'er Bethlehem it took its rest;
And there it did both stop and stay,
Right over the place where Jesus lay.

Refrain.

Then did they know assuredly
Within that house the King did lie;
One enter'd it them for to see,
And found the Babe in poverty.

Refrain.

Then entered in those wisemen three,
Full reverently upon the knee,
And offered there, in His presence,
Their gold and myrrh and frankincense.

Refrain.

Between an ox-stall and an ass,
This Child truly there He was;
For want of clothing they did him lay
All in a manger, among the hay.

Refrain.

Then let us all with one accord
Sing praises to our heav'nly Lord;
That hath made heaven and earth of naught,
And with His blood mankind hath bought.

Refrain.

If we in our time shall do well,
We shall be free from death and hell;
For God hath prepared for us all
A resting place in general.

Refrain.

JOY TO THE WORLD!

Isaac Watts (1674-1748)

Joy to the world! the Lord is come;
Let earth receive her King;
Let ev'ry heart prepare Him room,
And heav'n and nature sing,
And heav'n and nature sing,
And heav'n, and heav'n and nature sing.

Joy to the world! the Savior reigns;
Let men their songs employ;
While fields and floods, rocks, hills and plains
Repeat the sounding joy,
Repeat the sounding joy,
Repeat, repeat the sounding joy.

He rules the world with truth and grace,
And makes the nations prove
The glories of His righteousness,
And wonders of His love,
And wonders of His love,
And wonders, and wonders of His love.

O COME, ALL YE FAITHFUL

John Francis Wade (1712-1786) John Reading (d. 1692)

O come, all ye faithful, joyful and triumphant,
O come ye, O come ye to Bethlehem;
Come and behold Him, born the king of angels;
O come, let us us adore Him,
O come, let us adore Him,
O come, let us adore Him, Christ, the Lord!

Sing, choirs of angels, sing in exultation,
O sing, all ye citizens of heaven above!
Glory to God, all glory in the highest;
O come, let us adore Him,
O come, let us adore Him,
O come, let us adore Him, Christ, the Lord!

Yea, Lord, we greet Thee, born this happy
morning,
Jesus, to Thee be all glory giv'n;
Word of the Father, now in flesh appearing;
O come, let us us adore Him,
O come, let us us adore Him,
O come, let us adore Him, Christ, the Lord!

GOD REST YOU MERRY, GENTLEMEN

Traditional English

God rest you merry, gentlemen,
Let nothing you dismay,
Remember Christ our Saviour
Was born on Christmas Day;
To save us all from Satan's pow'r
When we were gone astray.

Refrain: O tidings of comfort and joy, comfort and joy;
O tidings of comfort and joy.

In Bethlehem in Jewry
This blessed Babe was born,
And laid within a manger,
Upon this blessed morn;
The which His mother Mary
Did nothing take in scorn.

Refrain.

From God our heav'nly Father
A blessed angel came;
And unto certain shepherds
Brought tidings of the same;
How that in Bethlehem was born
The son of God by name.

Refrain.

"Fear not, then," said the angel,
"Let nothing you affright,
This day is born a Saviour
Of a pure Virgin bright,
To free all those who trust in Him
From Satan's power and might."

Refrain.

The shepherds at those tidings
Rejoiced much in mind,
And left their flocks a-feeding,
In tempest, storm, and wind,
And went to Bethl'em straightway
This blessed Babe to find.

Refrain.

But when to Bethlehem they came,
Whereat this Infant lay,
They found Him in a manger,
Where oxen feed on hay;
His mother Mary kneeling,
Unto the Lord did pray.

Refrain.

Now to the Lord sing praises,
All you within this place,
And with true love and brotherhood
Each other now embrace;
This holy tide of Christmas
All others doth deface.

Refrain.

God bless the ruler of this house,
And send him long to reign,
And many a merry Christmas
May live to see again;
Among your friends and kindred
That live both far and near —
And God send you a happy new year,
  happy new year,
And God send you a happy new year.

GO TELL IT ON THE MOUNTAIN

Negro Spiritual

When I was a seeker,
I sought both night and day,
I sought the Lord to help me,
and He showed me the way.

Refrain: Oh! Go tell it on the mountain,
over the hills and everywhere,
Go tell it on the mountain
that Jesus Christ is born!

He made me a watchman
upon the city wall,
And if I am a Christian,
I am the least of all.

Refrain.

THE TWELVE DAYS OF CHRISTMAS

Traditional English

On the first day of Christmas
My true love sent to me:
A partridge in a pear tree.

On the second day of Christmas
My true love sent to me:
Two turtle doves,
And a partridge in a pear tree.

On the third day of Christmas
My true love sent to me:
Three French hens,
Two turtle doves,
And a partridge in a pear tree.

On the fourth day of Christmas
My true love sent to me:
Four calling birds,
Three French hens,
Two turtle doves,
And a partridge in a pear tree.

On the fifth day of Christmas
My true love sent to me:
Five gold rings,
Four calling birds,
Three French hens,
Two turtle doves,
And a partridge in pear tree.

On the sixth day of Christmas
My true love sent to me:
Six geese a-laying,
Five gold rings,
Four...(etc.)

...Seven swans a-swimming...
...Eight maids a-milking...
...Nine ladies dancing...
...Ten lords a-leaping...
...Eleven pipers piping...
...Twelve drummers drumming...

...And a partridge in a pear tree.

DECK THE HALLS WITH BOUGHS OF HOLLY

Traditional Welsh

Deck the halls with boughs of holy,
Fa-la-la-la-la, la-la-la-la;
'Tis the season to be jolly,
Fa-la-la-la-la, la-la-la-la.
Don we now our gay apparel,
Fa-la-la, fa-la-la, la-la-la.
Troll the ancient Christmas carol,
Fa-la-la-la-la, la-la-la-la.

See the blazing yule before us,
Fa-la-la-la-la, la-la-la-la.
Strike the harp and join the chorus,
Fa-la-la-la-la, la-la-la-la.
Follow me in merry measure,
Fa-la-la, fa-la-la, la-la-la.
While I tell of Christmas treasure,
Fa-la-la-la-la, la-la-la-la.

Fast away the old year passes,
Fa-la-la-la-la, la-la-la-la.
Hail the new, ye lads and lasses,
Fa-la-la-la-la, la-la-la-la.
Sing we joyous songs together,
Fa-la-la, fa-la-la, la-la-la.
Heedless of the wind and weather,
Fa-la-la-la-la, la-la-la-la.

JINGLE BELLS

John Pierpont (1785-1866)

Dashing through the snow,
In a one-horse open sleigh,
O'er the fields we go,
Laughing all the way;
Bells on bob-tail ring,
Making spirits bright,
What fun it is to ride and sing
A sleighing song tonight!

Jingle bells, jingle bells,
Jingle all the way!
Oh, what fun it is to ride
In a one-horse open sleigh!
Jingle bells, jingle bells,
Jingle all the way!
Oh, what fun it is to ride
In a one-horse open sleigh!

OTHER BOOKS
BY CHERI FULLER

Motivating Your Kids
From Crayons to Career

Home-Life
The Key to Your Child's
Success at School

Available from your local bookstore
or by writing:

HONOR

P. O. Box 55388
Tulsa, Oklahoma 74155-1388

Cheri Fuller, born in Dallas, Texas, was the fourth of six children. Home was a place where something interesting was always happening. Even as a small child, she remembers the art time, nature walks, backyard games, and playing school at home with her sisters. Because of these experiences, she learned to read before starting school. In the course of family life, she also began writing — long letters to grandparents and to an uncle who lived in Alaska, poems for birthday cards, and verses for special occasions.

Cheri has had extensive experience in teaching English and creative writing. She taught freshman composition at the university level, an inner city catch-up program for disadvantaged youth, public junior high, private college preparatory school, Christian elementary, junior high, and high school.

She also taught history and world geography. She has privately tutored, teamtaught, and written cirriculum.

Through her teaching experience, she developed a concern for the sliding academic skills she saw in the classroom and wanted to use her experience to help parents provide an environment supportive to learning. This led her to research the causes and solutions to the school problems and to write a book for parents. She teaches workshops for parent groups and PTA's on topics such as learning style, encouraging reading and writing skills, and other topics, and teaches in the classroom young authors' workshops to encourage their writing skills.

Cheri holds a bachelor's degree in English, history, and secondary education, and a Master's degree in English Literature from Baylor University in Waco, Texas. She and her husband Holmes have three children: Justin, Chris and Alison.

To contact Cheri Fuller,
write:

Cheri Fuller
P. O. Box 770493
Oklahoma City, Oklahoma 73177